THE COMPLETE SMALL BUSINESS LOAN KIT

CONSUMER LAW FOUNDATION

- SBA loan opportunities for your business
  - How to set up the best package with public or private institutions
  - Your winning business plan
- Presentations that get results
- A-1 Credit — easier than you think
- International trade assistance
- Information on special programs for veterans, the handicapped and minorities

BOB ADAMS, INC.
PUBLISHERS

ACKNOWLEDGMENTS

I wish to thank the Boston office of the Small Business Administration for valuable assistance in the preparation of this book. The guidance and insights into SBA loan procedures I garnered from this institution have helped make this book a useful tool to loan applicants. Special thanks are also due to Al Cook and the Lazarus Corporation, for input on the section on business plans. Finally, I am indebted to my wife Marlene for her assistance in the preparation of the manuscript; without her patience and tireless efforts, this book never would have reached completion.

Arnold Goldstein
Consumer Law Foundation

Information contained in this book has been carefully compiled from sources believed to be reliable, but the accuracy of the information is not guaranteed, as laws and regulations may change ot be subject to differing interpretations.

This book is sold with the understanding that neither the author nor the publisher is engaged in rendering legal advice. If legal advice is required, the services of a competent attorney should be sought.

Published by Bob Adams, Inc., 260 Center Street, Holbrook, MA 02343.

ISBN 1-55850-996-8

Printed in the United States of America.

CONTENTS

About This Book

By correctly assembling a few facts and figures, almost any small business owner can become eligible for many different types of loans. This book shows how to gather and prepare the needed information.

Much of what is covered here concerns loans through the Small Business Administration; however, private sources are also discussed in detail. *The Complete Small Business Loan Kit* is a valuable business resource that will be helpful in your efforts to secure loans from both banks and governmental sources. Where appropriate, essential forms (properly completed) have been reproduced in their entirety.

It is recommended that you read the book through completely before initiating any loan application. By reviewing the facts and requirements beforehand--presented here in clear, easy-to-understand terms--you'll avoid costly mistakes that may cause your loan to be denied.

Section One:
The Basics

CHAPTER ONE:
Preparing a Winning Business Plan

A well-prepared business plan is essential when dealing with prospective lenders. The first thing lenders look for is a complete, concise and thorough business plan. If you are serious about obtaining your business loan, you will spend a great deal of time assembling these materials.

The sad truth is that most people strategize their business ventures poorly. A realistic business plan can help you avoid the pitfalls that take other small businesses under. The following sections will show how you can develop a sound business plan, and detail its value as a management tool.

HOW A PLAN CAN HELP YOU

The process of creating a business plan forces you to take a realistic, objective and detached look at your business in its entirety. Most people who have business ideas deal with them in an unorganized manner, often putting out one "fire" at a time. Putting a business plan together with specifics provides you the opportunity to evaluate your business as a whole, and in more concrete terms than you are likely to use if you concentrate only on the firm's day-to-day problems.

A finished business plan becomes an operating tool that will help you manage your business and work toward its success. The final, completed plan is the chief tool for communicating your ideas to others--potential lenders, other businesspeople, bankers, partners, etc. If you seek financing for your business, the plan will become the foundation for your loan proposal.

Moreover, by taking an objective look at your business, you can identify areas of strength and weakness. You can pinpoint your needs or examine problems you might normally overlook. A business plan will give you enough information to help you spot problems before they arise.

Planning helps you: identify precise objectives; develop clear strategies to meet those objectives; red-flag problems and suggest ways to solve them; and create or reinforce a structure for your business by defining activities and responsibilities. Last but not least, of course, your plan will help you obtain the necessary financing to start your business.

A business plan, after all, provides information needed by others who will evaluate your venture. There are many types of lenders or investors, but you will get money from them only by making them confident that your business is going to be secure and profitable. Keep in mind that lenders have not been thinking about your business as you have. They are seeing it on paper for the first time. You must therefore present something to them that clearly, succinctly, and reasonably gives them confidence you're going to make (not lose) money.

Here, as elsewhere in business, it is important to view things from the other person's perspective. Large lenders usually aren't anxiously looking around for small businesses to finance. Unfortunately, most small-business owners seldom have the time or financial expertise to present their ideas to the right sources, or to package their business in a manner that will convince lenders to finance them. Whatever kind of lender you eventually find, SBA or private, you're going to have to present a cogent business plan, one that addresses the concerns and doubts of the person from whom you'd like to borrow money.

There is a positive cycle you can initiate by preparing a strong business plan, a cycle that tends to reinforce itself. Once you thoroughly research and put your business plan together, you are likely to obtain an enormous amount of financial and operational information about your business. Information promotes business knowledge and confidence; confidence, in turn, promotes enthusiasm, and makes you a convincing advocate for your business.

The bottom line is that if you're going to use your business plan for the purpose of raising money, you must be able to sell your idea, your plan, and your business enthusiastically. If you don't know everything about your program, you're not going to be the salesperson you must be. This doesn't mean you must necessarily be a superior salesperson, in the everyday sense of the phrase, to obtain financing. Nevertheless, the owner of any business must be able to talk convincingly about benefits and risks to a lender, and must be able to field questions in an intelligent and straightforward manner. Fortunately, with some work and persistence, anyone can achieve this level of knowledge and confidence.

You must take adequate time to put your plan together correctly. Some people take weeks, others months. If you work full-time, you'll find it's almost impossible to put a plan together quickly. In this case, it's best to have a sound plan that takes a while to assemble, rather than a poor one that you complete in short order.

A well-organized plan will tell you if your business idea makes sense. It can reveal whether there is enough net profit in a business to make it an enterprise worth time or investment and hence whether it makes sense to pursue. It is clear enough that this is information you must have in order to make your business a successful one. Accordingly, you should take whatever time you feel is necessary to develop a sound plan.

A business plan also forces you to analyze your market, not only from your point of view as a business operator, but also from the potential customer's point of view. You must determine the potential demand for the product or service you plan to offer. Additionally, you must evaluate your particular ability to competitively provide the product or service. Therefore, a business plan will disclose whether your idea has a reasonable chance of succeeding in the marketplace. It is entirely possible that an idea for which you have great enthusiasm is not sufficiently market-oriented. Do your best to maintain objectivity.

Finally, a business plan can also help you decide whether you're physically, mentally, and emotionally capable of taking on the challenge of setting up, running, and operating a business over the long term. Many people are not, and you will save yourself a great deal of time, work, and aggravation if you reach this conclusion now, rather than several years from now.

STRUCTURING THE BUSINESS PLAN

A well-written business plan is comprehensive, with information grouped into logical sections. It should be extremely easy to read. After all, you want your reader concentrating on the potential profitability of your ideas, not struggling to understand them in the first place. The final product should feature no sudden reversals or extravagant leaps from one point to another.

In short, the plan should hold few surprises for its reader. It should conform to generally accepted guidelines of form and content. Aside from introductory material, your plan should probably have between ten and thirteen sections. Each section should include specific elements that will clarify your business goals.

The points that must be addressed by your plan are outlined on the following pages.

Statement of purpose and summary.

General description of business.

Market analysis.

Market strategy.

Design and development plans.

Operations plan.

Management structure.

Timetables and schedules.

Financial data.

Supporting information.

SBA materials (if applicable).

(*Note:* the various sections may be organized according to the following outline.)

1. Cover Page

   A. Name of company and status

   B. Address

   C. Phone number

   D. Submitted to . . . (personalized for each lender)

   E. Prepared by . . . (or: person to contact)

2. Purpose and Summary

   A. Company name and type

   B. Amount of financing needed

   C. How the money will be used

   D. Impact of financing on the business

   E. How the plan will be implemented

3. Description of the Business

   A. Industry

   B. Specific type of business

   C. Products or services

   D. Age and growth

   E. Success factors

4.   Market Analysis

   A. Customers

   B. Market size and trends

   C. Competition

   D. Estimated market share and sales

   E. Market opportunities

5.   Marketing Strategy

   A. Overall plan

   B. Pricing

   C. Sales

   D. Customer service

   E. Distribution

   F. Advertising and promotion

6.   Design and Development Plans

   A. Product status

   B. Development risks

   C. Product improvement and new products

   D. Impact on business

7.   Operations Plan

   A. Location

   B. Equipment needs

   C. Distribution

   D. Personnel

8. Management Structure
   A. Organization
   B. Key personnel and background
   C. Compensation
   D. Professional advisors

9. Timetables and Schedules
   A. Growth plans
   B. Overall schedule

10. Financial Information
    A. Personal capital to be invested
    B. Application of proceeds
    C. Break-even analysis
    D. Balance sheet
    E. Pro forma two-year cash flow analysis
    F. Pro forma five-year profit and loss statement

For Existing Businesses (additional):
    A. Current audited financial statement
    B. Tax returns for prior three years
    C. Any other significant historical information

11. Supporting Information
    A. Letters of intent, recommendation
    B. Purchase orders
    C. Job descriptions
    D. Newspaper and magazine clippings
    E. Special awards, achievements

(SBA forms and documents may be included in the above section if you are applying for an SBA loan. Consult your local bank officer or SBA personnel for guidelines.)

RESEARCH AND GOAL-SETTING

It's important to prepare yourself well to develop your business plan. This usually means intensive research.

You must think about what kind of business you have, what you need, and what is critical to your business and your overall goals, targets, and objectives. Be sure, for example, to note not only how much financing will be needed, but also when.

Be specific about time when you describe your targets. Be clear about the scope and limit of your business. Do not overemphasize one part of the business at the expense of others. If your plan is oriented toward operations, be sure to explain your goals for research and development, engineering, manufacturing, and distribution as well. Then consider your marketing: your advertising, promotion, and sales force. In general, ask yourself the tried-and-true questions: who, what, where, when, why, and how. Then add another query: how much.

You should do your research before you begin writing your plan. Start by gathering a range of information about your industry category in general, and the business in particular. Keep an open mind; you may shift your business emphasis as you come across important facts.

Talk to others in the business you plan to enter. Of course, you should choose businesses that wouldn't be directly competitive with yours. Perhaps they serve a distant geographic area or sell products or services to a market slightly different from yours. This network is often difficult to establish. You may have to call several people before finding one who will discuss business candidly.

Trade associations serving your industry are as near as your telephone, and can be a great help. Many such organizations publish trade magazines or journals. You can find associations suited to your needs by checking the Encyclopedia of Associations, found in most libraries.

When preparing your plan, it's important to give yourself time and privacy so you can think creatively. Once you have gathered information and know quite a bit about your business, give yourself sufficient time to digest the facts and develop a sound strategy.

This is the time to set up your planning goals, objectives, and targets, and to develop your marketing outline, operations outline, and financial materials. You must decide what kind of money you'll require, when you're going to borrow it, and the time frame you'll need to break even.

WRITING THE BUSINESS PLAN

Once you have made enough headway with the research and goal-setting work, you'll be ready to begin writing. Do not assume that you must write each section of the business plan in the same order in which it will appear in the final product. It's likely that you will get more quality work done by attacking topics independently, and assembling the material in the proper sequence later.

Of course, your business plan should have a cover--neat and of adequate size.

Include a title page in your business plan. On this plan, put the name of the business and the names of the principals who own it, as well as a business address and phone number. If you have a professional, businesslike logo, use it to dress up your title page. Personalize the cover for the particular lender to whom it will be presented.

Next comes the statement of purpose and summary. The summary should give the reader an overview of what you want, and is extremely important. All too often, the financing needs are buried in the middle of the report, making it difficult for prospective lenders to evaluate the plan properly. Make quite clear what you are asking for in the summary.

The summary should state the nature of the business, the legal form of operation (sole proprietorship, partnership, corporation, or limited partnership), the amount and purpose of the loan being requested, the repayment schedule requested, the equity contributed by the borrower, and the equity-debt ratio after the loan, security, or collateral is offered.

Make it easy for prospective lenders to learn your wants and capabilities. Remember: businesspeople in general, and successful businesspeople in particular, tend to be short on time. If you can get to a yes or no decision promptly, you will waste neither your time nor the time of the lender.

Whether the plan is to be used for financial or operations purposes, its statement of purpose should outline your financial goals and requirements, and should be kept short and businesslike, usually no more than a page. (Only in special settings, such as an extremely large loan or a complicated use of funds, should your summary be longer.) One approach is to put a broad outline of the material in your statement of purpose in paragraph form, and then, on the page following, include a table that shows how loan proceeds will be distributed, as well as the source and use of the funds. As you prepare your first draft of the statement of purpose, you will probably realize that it cannot be completed with actual numbers until you've calculated your capital needs. But you can write a draft version, leave the numbers blank, and complete it later.

Following the statement of purpose comes a table of contents. Of course, you will prepare this last, but be aware that you do need to include one. When you or others look over your plan, you should be able to find specific information quickly. Note that the table of contents does not appear at the very beginning of the plan. This is an important point; you must give the reader some idea of the business's direction in the summary before presenting potentially confusing numbers and facts. Once the business is summarized and the reader knows what you want, it will be easier for him to read the entire plan or turn to a section of interest.

With this much completed, you are ready to begin assembling the core of your plan.

THE DESCRIPTION OF THE BUSINESS

Is the business a middle-of-the-road concept or specialized? Is it a startup, a franchise, or an expansion? Describe the industry in which your business will be involved, as well as the present outlook for the industry. Discuss all the various markets within the industry, including any new developments that will benefit or adversely affect your business.

Classify your business and note whether it is a wholesale, retail, manufacturing, recycling, or service-oriented operation. Outline the status of the business--existing or new--and its form, whether sole proprietorship, limited partnership, or corporation.

Describe an existing business thoroughly. Detail when it started, who started it, why they are selling, and how you can improve the business.

State the business operating days and hours. Mention seasonal fluctuations and how you will address the manpower variations and other pitfalls you may encounter.

You needn't prepare an exhaustive, twenty-page description of the products or service concept you intend to market, but you should give a good, broad overview of what you want to do and the environment in which you'll do it.

MARKET ANALYSIS

By conducting a thorough market survey, you can obtain the information necessary for a market analysis. Many published sources provide market-related information; there may be a statistical study available through the business branch of your local library that offers exactly what you need to know about the business you're planning. Whatever sources you consult, try to establish for yourself how complete, accurate, and specific they are to your needs. Typically, one informational source will lead you to more. Find and use the ones that are best suited to your requirements.

Possible non-library sources include: government reports; advertising agency publications; market research firms; and banks. After you've checked out these secondary sources, you may consider whether you need to do your own direct market research.

Describe your customer base. Who are the potential customers for your product or service? Where are they located? What are their characteristics? What is the size of your market? What percentage of that market is or will be yours? How will you attract and keep your market share?

Research your market. Specify the aggregate market statistics (or consumer demographics) your business will face. These can often be found in trade publications and other published accounts of the industry. Discuss the growth potential of your specific market.

Once you've determined that your market is adequate to support your business and make it profitable, check out your competition. List your four or five nearest competitors, as well as their business addresses.

Observing your competition is often a better source of information than any library or consultant. You can see first hand how the industry operates by watching how those in your business area face challenges. The information you'll gain as a result is useful not only to those who will be reading and evaluating your plan, but also to you.

Answer the important questions. How do your competitors' operations differ from the one you plan? How can yours improve upon theirs? How successful are their businesses? Talk to their suppliers. Talk to their customers. Is the operation in question steady? Is it increasing or decreasing? Why? What are the players' strengths and weaknesses? How are their weaknesses working to your advantage? What can you do to take advantage of those weaknesses?

Your goal is to show the lender how your business will differ from your competition, and how your operation will give you greater profits. You may decide to imitate, or you may improve on your competition while avoiding their errors. Tell why and how you will do so. As you discuss your competition, reveal one or two businesses that aren't doing well. Rather than scare a lender, this will show you're a realist, and recognize that some businesses don't do as well as others. Such a tactic represents an opportunity for you to show how you will correct the mistakes of others.

Be specific in showing how you will give your business a competitive edge. Point out, for example, that your business will be better because you will supply a full line of products; competitor A doesn't have a full line. Alternatively, you might argue that you're going to provide service after the sale; competitor B doesn't service what he sells. There are many such points you can make: your merchandise will be of higher quality; you'll give a money-back guarantee; you'll provide parts and labor for up to 90 days after the sale. Remember, your company must offer a competitive advantage if it is to penetrate an already competitive market.

MARKET STRATEGY

If your market research has been completed properly, you should have at your fingertips the foundation for your strategy. It should begin with a brief summary of your marketing analysis and should cover a minimum of three years.

The overall plan sets the marketing policy. It will convey to the lender exactly how you will proceed with your marketing effort, what tactics will be employed, and what is different about your business--what will contribute to its success in the marketplace.

The reader will also want information about your pricing in this section of the plan. Many factors will influence your pricing strategies, including your competitors' prices and the type of operation you have. Is the business a wholesale outlet? A retail store? If it is a retail store, is it targeted toward an "upscale" market, or to a more price-sensitive segment?

It's important to be knowledgeable about pricing structures in your industry, and to be able to justify convincingly your pricing policies.

Provide short-term as well as long-term plans. Give examples of your competitors' pricing practices. If it is appropriate to give a broad overview of your commission structure, you can do so here.

A selling schedule and sales budget will come in handy in this section. It will help illustrate when sales will begin, delivery time, marketing costs, and any projected slowdowns.

Outline, if appropriate, your customer service policies, including details on return policies, warranty periods, or guarantees. Depending on the type of business you enter, such factors may be of great importance to your marketing efforts, or of no consequence whatsoever.

To round out your marketing efforts, describe the most appropriate forms of advertising; discuss the kinds of promotions you plan to execute. Advertising and promotion are important to any business; your goal is to expose your product or service to a wide range of potential customers in a compelling way.

You don't have to detail the exact costs of specific advertisements in this section, but you should provide an estimated advertising budget and a breakdown of the various media you will utilize in your advertising campaign.

DESIGN AND DEVELOPMENT PLANS

If you have already developed a product or service concept and have all the components at a point you consider marketable, this section won't be necessary.

If you do need to complete this section, explain exactly what your product or service is, what it is designed to do, and what needs to be done to make it marketable. In addition, review the costs associated with production or service delivery, proposed schedules, and any foreseeable problems.

If you have developed the idea but not the product, have plans to improve and existing product, or are an existing company with plans to introduce a new product, this section is extremely important to the business plan. Your reader will want to know the development progress of any product or service concept, the costs associated with delivering a marketable item, and reasons to believe it can be done in the period of time you outline.

OPERATIONS PLAN

Your primary objective in the operations section is to describe how you will conduct your business. Discuss what will be required in terms of location of the physical plant, necessary equipment, and the purchase and management of inventory.

This part of the business plan must reflect your overall philosophy and policy structure for the business. Anyone lending money is going to be looking for consistency, and the basis for that consistency should be evident in the description of how the business will run.

Include a thorough location analysis. This is essential to a strong business plan. Begin the analysis by stating exactly where you plan to establish your business (or where it is presently located if yours is an ongoing operation). Note the community within which the business will be located and the limits of the geographic area the business will serve.

Give a detailed account of the operational strategies that will make your business run. If yours is a manufacturing business, provide information that describes all the procedures at every level of production and distribution. If the business is a retail operation, outline the purchasing and retail process. The service procedures should be detailed closely if yours is a service concept.

Be sure to include subjects such as inventory financing, available labor, and your relationship with key vendors.

Discuss the wages you plan to pay for inexperienced and/or experienced workers. Note whether you are going to use independent contractors or have people on payroll. If you use a commission schedule, what will it be? What employee benefits do you plan to offer? Be specific.

MANAGEMENT STRUCTURE

Include a chart illustrating the key positions within the management of the company; detail who will fill each post. Elaborate upon each individual's past experience and any work experience with other management personnel. Basically, your task here is to provide job descriptions of those closest to the business. Clarifying who does what, where, how, and why is essential for any business to run smoothly and profitably.

Complete resumes of each person on the management team should be included in an appendix to the plan.

Avoid extravagant executive salaries! If, at the outset of a venture, you include extremely high salaries for yourself and/or your management team, the lender will conclude (and rightly so) that you and your management team lack the commitment to make the business a success.

OVERALL SCHEDULE

Include one or more schedules detailing the timetables for startup, expansion, and capital fund requirements. These schedules should show the timing and interrelationship of the major events necessary to launch your venture.

Highlight the start of the business and your expected growth over the next three years. Only novice entrepreneurs begin a business with no idea of how the business will evolve and what to do when it does. Clarify your strategy for dealing with growth. If you're starting a small hardware center within a department store and plan to grow to an independent houseware supply store within the next three years, detail how this expansion and transition will take place. You'll need more space, more money, more inventory, and more support personnel; let the lender know how these items will come together for future growth.

The schedule should also include any deadlines or major events that are critical to the success of the business.

FINANCIAL INFORMATION

Because the financial data is so important, it will be discussed separately in the following chapter.

SUPPORTING INFORMATION

Finally, there is a catch-all section for your supporting information. This is the section that allows you to dress up your business, and even to display a measure of charm, personality and creativity. Think of all your supporting documentation as icing on the cake. But remember: the documents you supply must be relevant (in other words, a photocopy of your high school diploma should be avoided). For best results, consider this section as a marketing tool.

If, for example, you have commitments from prospective clients, include their letters of intent to do business with you. In-hand purchase orders might be equally effective exhibits.

You should include several letters of reference from people who know you. These can be business or community leaders, friends, or business associates. A reference letter should be short, indicating how long the person has known you and in what capacity.

Other items that can be included in your supporting documents include patents, census or demographic data, insurance requirements, license requirements, or anything else you feel evidences the potential success of your business.

SBA MATERIAL

If you are applying for a Small Business Administration loan, you'll include all relevant SBA data (outlined later on in this book), keeping in mind that your SBA materials should be thought of as an adjunct to your plan. Also remember that neatness counts, and that it is the job of an SBA loan official (or any other bureaucrat) to pigeonhole, quantify, or otherwise categorize those he deals with. Make life easy for everyone; be sure the material demonstrates how organized, concise, and easy to deal with you really are.

CHAPTER TWO:
Finding
Professional
Assistance

Whether you are just starting a business, buying an existing business, or expanding a business you already own, you will face a variety of financing problems. You'll be able to solve many of them yourself without help. In some cases, however, you'll need the services of professionals. Your enterprise will not be unusual in this respect: most every business turns to experts for services at some point.

Financing is a specialty of its own; it is not unusual for an entrepreneur to turn to outsiders to locate suitable sources of financing, or to help in the preparation of loan documents. In fact, seeking outside help may be one of the smartest moves you can make; financing specialists can often help you obtain faster, lower cost loans than you could possibly obtain on your own. In this chapter we'll examine some of the most promising sources for outside help.

FREE HELP FROM THE SBA

The Small Business Administration's best known and most widely used service is part of the Agency's Business Development Program. You may already be familiar, in fact, with SCORE (the Service Corps of Retired Executives) and ACE (the Active Corps of Executives). These organizations are sponsored by the SBA to help small business executives solve operating problems through free one-on-one counselling. Through SCORE and ACE, small business owners and managers can receive expert help from seasoned executives who, in most cases, have experience in the field of business they advise on.

Although SCORE and ACE personnel do not directly assist in the preparation of SBA applications, their volunteer consultants can often provide valuable management advice essential to assembling a compelling financing proposal.

Small business owners can apply for assistance from SBA by completing a simple "Request for Counseling" form and forwarding it to the nearest SBA field office. (See the appendix for a directory.) Assistance is available in a number of problem areas, including starting a new business, international trade, recordkeeping and accounting, personnel, and market research. When requesting SBA assistance, fill out SBA Form 641, describing the kind of help you need. As discussed in detail later in this book, management assistance is also available through Small Business Institutes, or SBIs, organized on nearly 500 college and university campuses across the country.

For further information contact: Small Business Answer Desk, SBA Advocacy Office, Room 403, 1441 "L" Street, N.W., Washington, D.C. 20416, (806) 368-5855.

YOUR ATTORNEY AND ACCOUNTANT

The Small Business Administration, of course, is limited in the assistance it can provide loan applicants and others. Help from other sources is sometimes necessary; often, those sources are attorneys or certified public accountants.

Many inexperienced businesspeople are reluctant to hire a lawyer or accountant because of the expense involved. But these professionals can be as important to a small business as to a national conglomerate, and costs are often returned many times over in time and money saved. Accountants and attorneys usually can be hired on an hourly basis, which allows you to control your expenditures in this area.

Many attorneys and accountants specialize in the problems of small businesses and are experienced in financing strategies that will work for you. Try to select professionals who have been recommended to you, and who have the background necessary to understand your problems.

Attend your first meeting prepared to question the professional in detail. Find out the names of businesses in your community with whom the professional works. Ask for descriptions of the types of services provided.

Make no commitment during your first visit. Instead, contact the owners of the businesses for whom the professional works and ask for references. Ask specific questions. Are the professional's charges reasonable? Are services provided on a timely basis? What difficulties have been experienced? Would he or she use the same professional again? Some cities have referral services that will bring a client and a layer or CPA together. These can be good sources of information. Often, however, they are sponsored by professional organizations and make recommendations of all members on a rotational basis without regard to practitioner specialties or backgrounds, and thus are not always the most reliable source of good leads. Admittedly, the process of finding the right professional counselors can take time, but it's almost always worth the effort.

Your accountant and your attorney will, of course, play very different roles as you prepare your loan application. Your accountant's responsibility will be largely confined to the preparation of the financial documents necessary to support your loan proposal. Your attorney's primary mission is to protect you from crucial errors on the loan documents. There are areas, however, where they may share responsibility, including deciding tax questions, or determining how a loan should be structured.

PROFESSIONAL LOAN PACKAGERS

Did you know that there are people who earn their livelihood from preparing loan proposals for clients? A significant share of their work is preparing SBA loan applications.

A professional SBA loan packager (not to be confused with an SBA loan officer) completes packages for startups, existing enterprises, and franchise opportunities needing a guaranteed loan. The ultimate goal is to reduce the amount of work that you or your staff must perform on this task.

Banks often refer applicants to these specialists. The point at which you may be referred to a loan packaging service depends on the lending institution. One lender may initially send you to a packager; another may wait to see whether you present the proposal in a professional manner on your own.

Occasionally, a franchisor and packager work together to develop a lender source. They then retain this same lending service throughout the franchisee lending process.

According to professional packagers, the most difficult aspect of the process is deciding how much money to apply for. Most people don't really know how much they need or are entitled to. If you are immersed in the day-to-day crises of your own business, you may not know what the business can realistically justify in terms of a loan amount. By the same token, it is difficult to know how much to borrow for a startup or an expansion loan. The packager can assist you in establishing your borrowing level.

Projections are the most complicated form of the financing proposal. Determining reasonably accurate monthly cash flow levels comes with experience; it is here the packager may offer the most important assistance.

As a matter of practice, the packager is often called in to complete both the lender's portion for the guarantee as well as the applicant's section of the loan package. Prior to submission to the local SBA office, the bank studies the applicant's credit information and includes this information in the loan package.

An experienced packager can recognize your strengths and weaknesses, and can offer suggestions and support in those areas that need attention. The loan packaging service should have a consultant with an established rapport with bank personnel; most packagers have completed enough loans to know which local bank specializes in the type of loan you require.

Some rules are interpreted slightly differently in different regions throughout the country. The packager will know if your SBA office tends to be more lenient toward a 10-year commercial real estate loan rather than a 20-year loan.

Loan packaging agents and firms can be found in most major metropolitan areas. Not surprisingly, many of these independent businessmen are former SBA employees. If you choose their services, bear in mind that they must complete a written agreement with you (SBA Form 159) and comply with the SBA regulations concerning compensation.

Each and every person retained by you to perform any service in connection with your loan application must complete and sign the appropriate SBA documentation. Take Form 159 with you when you visit the packager's office so the form can be completed immediately after your negotiations. (All of the documentation associated with SBA loans is discussed in detail later in this book.)

Of course, loan packagers are usually equally capable of preparing proposals for commercial banks. Check with your potential packager and determine his or her level of experience in packaging your type of loan.

PROFESSIONALLY PREPARED BUSINESS PLANS

The business plan is the most complicated part of the loan application, and the area in which you are most likely to need professional assistance. If, after reviewing the material in the previous chapter, you feel you aren't up to the task, you still have some options.

You can opt to have your business plan professionally prepared: researched, written, and printed by outsiders. But there are pros and cons to this practice. While a knowledgeable consultant can be an extremely useful advisor to anyone contemplating financing for a business, don't think you can "farm out" everything connected with the plan. If you wish to make a profit in your business--to control its operation and manage it efficiently--you must understand every word, every dollar amount, and every item in the plan. You must be accountable for every penny and every paragraph of any plan you submit to a banker, an SBA loan officer, or a venture capitalist.

Why? At some point your consultant is going to move on. You will have to stay with your business, on your own, and run it yourself. Or you will have to make your own financing presentation by yourself. These lenders are going to be taking a good look at you, and are going to be asking you questions. If you have to look to your consultant to answer fundamental inquiries, neither you nor your business prospects are going to be viewed favorably.

In the planning phase of your business, it's particularly advisable to do the work yourself. Even if you're not a writer, you must nevertheless be the principal supplier of data to the writer who puts your information into the business plan. If you can explain the concept of your business to someone who needs to understand it in order to put your plan into final form, then the chances are good that you will be able to make lenders and others understand it as well. In any case, remember that understanding comes from being involved with your business idea from the beginning.

There are companies that will organize and write a business plan for you. They will charge you from several hundred dollars up to $10,000 for their services; you will receive a very professional and polished plan for your money. But a business plan becomes even more valuable when you devote the time to organize and write it yourself. It helps you to understand what your business is about and will make you a better manager when you're up and running. Just as you cannot expect your business to grow without your active involvement, neither can you expect a business plan to do much for you without your controlling its design.

Writing the business plan is not an insurmountable task if you truly understand your business venture. The bulk of the information is easy enough to obtain. The difficulty lies in digesting all the information, sorting out the pertinent data, and organizing those relevant pieces into a dynamic, challenging whole.

Where can you find the help you need? Try business professors at local universities. Many professionals "moonlight" as business plan preparers. You might also ask your local banker. Lenders see hundreds of business plans each year, and can usually tell you who in your area provides the best service. Don't forget your accountant or attorney--they are invaluable sources, not only for information and advice, but also for industry contacts.

CHAPTER THREE:
How to Build
A-1 Credit

A surprising number of people are turned down for financing because they lack a good credit rating. Good credit, in fact, is the backbone of successful borrowing. Without acceptable credit your loan application has no chance of approval, no matter how sound your application for a loan may be in other areas.

For this reason you must check your credit rating (and correct any problems) well before you apply for financing.

HOW TO REPAIR POOR CREDIT

Good credit is essential for most of us; many of the things we want to buy require some sort of financing. However, once you acquire a bad credit rating, it is nearly impossible to avoid detection when you apply for financing. An extensive network of credit reporting agencies keep track of a bewildering number of credit applicants. Each time you apply for credit through a bank, store or credit card agency, the prospective lender can be counted on to check your credit with one or more of these agencies before issuing you credit.

There are nearly 2000 credit bureaus in the United States, but there are only a few large regional bureaus. The top five are TRW, Transunion, Chilton, CBI, and Pinger. TRW, the largest, has approximately 80 million credit files in storage, processes over 30 million credit reports a year, and has 35,000 business subscribers.

Many businesses pay to obtain credit information contained in bureau files. Such subscribers believe, with justification, that the information contained in the credit file is a good indication of a person's creditworthiness. After all, it does make sense to assume that how you have paid other creditors in the past is an indication of how you may act in the future. Subscribers also use the credit file to verify information on credit applications.

As a rule, the same potential creditors that receive information about you also provide information to the credit bureaus. When you fill out an application for a credit account, the information is likely to be forwarded to the bureau; similarly, updates on the status of your account are typically sent to the bureau to keep your file up to date.

Not all creditors report everything they know to the credit bureaus. And of those who do, not all report the whole contents of their file.

Creditors most likely to be in contact with credit bureaus in this way are commercial banks, (including the credit card departments), most other credit card firms, larger savings and loans institutions, major department stores, and finance companies.

Accounts that are usually *not* reported include those with utilities, hospitals, and credit unions, as well as oil company credit cards. Mortgage and checking/savings account information is not often reported to the bureaus, which means there is little chance of a bounced check or two scuttling one's loan application.

WHAT YOUR CREDIT REPORT DISCLOSES

Credit reports may vary slightly between agencies. However, most credit reports include:

Identification information. Your full name, last two addresses, social security number, date of birth, and place of employment if that information is available. Often, it is not, which can lead to critical misinterpretations. A creditor may reject an application when confronted with a credit report that "can't confirm employment," though the applicant is, unbeknownst to the creditor, gainfully employed at a new job. Similarly, if you are self-employed, that information may be rendered as "unemployed." The important topic of how to correct these and other possible errors is addressed below.

Detailed information on the accounts that are listed. This includes the name of the issuer, the date the account was opened, the original balance or limit, the current balance (beginning with the reporting date, which is also listed), the terms, and the current status of the account. The status of each item is indicated by means of a complicated code system; little room is left for guesswork. The terminology can make the matter of clearing your record difficult. Even if you are currently in the process of repaying a delinquent account, you are likely to be listed under an unflattering category. (For instance, "CO NOW PAY," which signifies a long-overdue balance considered "charged off"--"CO"-- that you are now repaying--"NOW PAY.")

Public record information. Information in this category might include bankruptcies, tax liens, judgments and other filings.

Credit report requests. Each time a creditor requests a copy of your report, this is recorded in your report and stays on for up to one year. This addition is "non-evaluated" by the bureau, but it can be seen as negative if you have many inquiries with no subsequent accounts opened. Creditors who see this activity will almost certainly assume you were turned down, even though there are other possible explanations for the inquiries.

Consumer statement. Finally, there is space on the report for you to place a consumer statement. This allows you to place 100 words explaining any situation in your profile to which you may disagree or feel needs some explanation.

FIVE COMMON REASONS FOR CREDIT DENIAL

When prospective lenders inquire about your credit standing, they examine your record with certain expectations. In order to evaluate your own report you need to know what those expectations are.

The most common reasons for credit denial (many of which are based on an analysis of a credit report) are listed below.

Delinquent credit obligations. Late payments, bad debts, or legal judgments against you make you look like a risky customer.

Credit application incomplete. Perhaps you left out some important information or made an error on the application. Any large discrepancy between your application and your credit file may cause the potential creditor to wonder if you are hiding something.

Too many inquiries. As noted above, inquiries are made whenever you apply for credit. Seeing your own report also counts as an inquiry, but is usually not held against you. Over a six-month period, as few as four inquiries may be considered to be a sign of excessive activity. The creditor may then presume that you are trying desperately to get credit, and are being rejected elsewhere.

Errors in your file. These may arise from typing mistakes, or from confusing your name with someone else's similar name. If you have changed your address, this can also create problems in the recording of your credit history. Since the credit bureaus handle millions of files, the possibility for error is always present. The only way errors can be found and corrected is by carefully reviewing your file for accuracy and taking the necessary steps to correct any problems you find.

Insufficient credit file. In other words, your "credit history" is too scanty for the type of credit you've requested. You probably need to develop your credit history more before qualifying for the level of credit you are requesting.

KNOWING WHAT'S ON YOUR REPORT

Whether or not you know of problems with your credit, you should examine your credit record before applying for credit. Periodic checking is important because credit bureaus can and do make mistakes in assembling credit information. As we've seen, they may confuse you with another individual or carry erroneous information in your file. They may even include false, incomplete or one-sided information provided by a creditor.

It is a good idea to get copies of your records from those bureaus that have a report on you. The addresses of local offices can be found in the Yellow Pages of your phone book under "credit" or "credit rating and reporting." If you cannot locate a local office, you can call a national credit bureau to obtain addresses of the local bureaus nearest you.

Call the organization and verify the exact fee for reviewing your file. Then write a letter to the local credit agency requesting a copy of your credit report. Include your own and your spouse's names, your current and previous address, your social security numbers, and your birthdates. With the letter enclose a check for the proper amount.

There are circumstances in which you are entitled to a free copy of your credit report. For example, if you have received a credit rejection within the past 30 days, you may enclose a copy of the rejection to the credit bureau listed on the rejection letter and demand that the agency provide a free copy of your credit report.

ASSERT YOUR LEGAL RIGHTS

What can you do if your credit report contains false, misleading or incomplete information?

The Fair Credit Reporting Act protects you against credit abuse that might result in unfair descriptions of your creditworthiness.

Knowing your rights is essential if you wish to erase the negative marks in your credit report and regain a good credit status. An overview of these rights follows.

You are allowed to challenge the accuracy of your credit report at any time; the credit bureau must "reinvestigate" anything you challenge, and it must do so within a reasonable period of time. The Federal Trade Commission defines "reasonable" as "immediately unless there is some good reason for the delay." For example, a delay might be caused by a large volume of inquiries to the agency at a particular time.

Your file must reflect corrections. If the credit bureau cannot confirm the adverse information, or if it finds any error, it must promptly delete the errone-ous information from its files.   If the bureau cannot or does not confirm the information you have challenged within a reasonable time period, it must also delete the information from your files.   If a creditor verifies the information, and the agency responds in a timely manner, the negative marks must remain on your record.   However . . .

If you maintain that the information reported is in dispute, you have the right to submit a Consumer Statement outlining your view of the problem.   In other words, if you as a credit consumer dispute the accuracy of certain informa-tion in your report and receive no satisfaction from the bureau or the creditor, then the credit bureau is required by law to attach your explanation (not to exceed 100 words) to every copy of the report it sends out.

REPAIRING YOUR CREDIT: A TEN STEP PLAN

With your credit report in hand, you are now ready to "repair" your credit rating.   Follow this ten step plan.

1. LOOK FOR NEGATIVE REMARKS

Find the negative remarks (also known as "dings") in your credit file and cir-cle them.   The information on these reports is usually coded like your bank statement.   However, the Fair Credit Reporting Act requires credit bureaus to explain anything on the report that you cannot reasonably be expected to under-stand.   You will find a key to the coding symbols.   Look for damaging remarks in four sections of your report:

> The *Historical Status* section is a record of your monthly payments.   Ide-ally, this should be free of "past due" symbols, which may reflect 30, 60, or 90 day delinquency periods.   In most cases, something like 90% of the negative remarks can be traced to "past due" symbols.   Many of these could be entered accidentally, or because the mails with your payment were late, or because of delays in processing payments.   Of course, you also may have actually made late payments.   Remember that you must have your payments credited to the account before the due date, not just mailed by that time, if you are to avoid late payment marks.

The *Comments* section may contain remarks such as "charged to P&L." "P&L" means "profit and loss." When a company charges an account to profit and loss, that means it has charged it off as a bad debt loss and that it does not expect to be able to collect. This, of course, implies that you are a bad credit risk.

The *Inquiries* section lists any queries made by any bank, store, or other company to which you applied for credit. "Too many" of these may be taken by a potential creditor as an indication that you are in financial difficulty and may be seeking credit as a solution. Creditors will often refer to give credit on the basis of "too many" inquiries. Nevertheless, what constitutes "too many" is a subjective judgment by the individual creditor.

Public Records can appear in your credit report. This category, as we've seen, may include tax liens, bankruptcies, or court judgments that affected you. These entries should also be examined closely for accuracy.

2. DETERMINE YOUR OVERALL CREDIT SCORE

Somewhere on your credit report you will find a column with a title such as "Account Profile." This column contains a summary rating for each of your accounts. A summary may read "positive," "negative," or "non-rated." "Positive" means you are a good credit risk; your payments are all on time. "Negative" means you have a serious credit problem; perhaps you have defaulted on a debt. "Non-rated" might mean you have a few late payments here and there. With a "non-rated" summary, you can still be in a weak position even though there is nothing strongly negative against you. Remember, each "negative" or "non-rated" entry has a code reflecting the nature of the problem. Your goal is to protest, and eventually remove, all profiles that are other than "positive."

3. DRAFT A PROTEST DISPUTING NEGATIVE ITEMS

Exercise your legal rights by aggressively challenging any bad marks. The credit bureau will only verify the facts if you assert that they are in error, so don't be shy! Draft a strong but polite protest for each item you want to challenge; state in the letter that you are exercising your rights under the Fair Credit Reporting Act, Section 611(b).

For example, suppose you find the code "Charge Off." This means that the creditor charged your account off to profit and loss. Usually, this indicates that the creditor thinks your debt is uncollectible. You could protest that this comment should be removed if the amount reflects a disputed debt, and the creditor in question was satisfied with the settlement you made. Or perhaps you eventually paid off the delinquent account in full, but the creditor failed to note this in your credit report.

Another problem might be a series of "Past Due" notations. You could protest that those payments were delayed due to a mixup with the post office when you changed your address. In response, the credit bureau and creditor will usually state that the payment was in fact late, and therefore it is correctly reported. However, if the mixup really did occur, you could submit a consumer statement to the effect that the account is in dispute because bills were not delivered by the creditor even though a change of address was furnished.

4. SEND YOUR LETTER OF DISPUTE

Write a letter of dispute to the credit bureau. Carefully detail each item you want to challenge. Be sure to include photocopies of any documents you provide to support your claims. These might include correspondence with your creditors, cancelled checks indicating payment, receipts, or other documents. Remember that the law states that you have the right to dispute any citation if the information contained in that citation is inaccurate or incomplete. (Section 611 of the Fair Credit Reporting Act.) The only limitation to this right is that your dispute should not be "frivolous or irrelevant."

5. RECORD YOUR ACTIONS

As soon as you mail the letter, log the date for each negative item you have protested. Keep related disputes together in a file with a copy of the letter, the credit report, and any other documents that you include with it.

6. WAIT "A REASONABLE TIME" FOR A RESPONSE

The waiting period will depend on several factors. Mark on your calendar the date you mail the letter. Try to get an estimate of the turnaround time from the bureau. Usually this period will be within four to eight weeks; you should not tolerate longer delays.

7. SEND A FOLLOW-UP LETTER

If the credit bureau does not respond within a reasonable time period, write a follow-up letter to the bureau reminding them of the estimated response time that they gave you.   Direct the letter to the person who gave you the estimate on the phone.   Point out that federal law requires that the credit bureau respond to a consumer dispute within a reasonable period of time, and that the agency is in violation of this law.

8. ASK FOR AN UPDATED CREDIT REPORT

At the end of the letter, or upon having your complaints addressed, ask for an updated copy of your credit report.   Section 611(d) of the Fair Credit Reporting Act requires the bureau to send a free notification of any updates to anyone who has received a copy of the report within six months previous to any corrections or statements that are added to the report.   Therefore, you are also entitled to receive a free update.   But you must request it in order to receive it, so be sure to make your request--and include a request to send an update to anyone else who has recently inquired about your credit.   (Note: the bureaus are not required to send a copy of the entire report, but they will often do so because that is more convenient for them.)

9. COMPARE THE NEW REPORT TO THE PRIOR REPORT

Compare the updated report to the original one.   Mark all improvements that you find.   Chances are, you will not get results on every protest the first time.   But some progress is likely.   The bureau may delete some items only because a creditor failed to respond to its investigation in a timely manner; this is a common occurrence.   The creditor's failure to deal with a bothersome piece of paperwork has now been turned to your advantage and is helping to clear your record.

10. REPEAT THE PROCESS

There are probably still some bad marks remaining; worse, it sometimes happens that a dispute results in an update to an account that is even more negative than before.   For example, reinvestigation could uncover the fact that you actually had more late payments than were previously reported.   What do you do?   Go back to the beginning of the process and start over again.   You should put your credit record through this process at least twice before going on to the next phase.   Remember that credit cannot be rebuilt in a day.   It takes patience and persistence.   Of course, during this process you must be very careful not to allow any new problems to show up on your record.   Be sure to keep all your accounts current or ahead of schedule.

GAINING CREDITOR COOPERATION

Many negative remarks cannot be deleted without creditor cooperation because the "dings" are accurate, and the creditor cooperates with the bureau's request for verification. Your goal here will be to soften the creditor's stance by either toning down or deleting entirely the remarks on your credit report. We will first address the issue of those creditors who were paid late, but who are no longer owed money.

SET UP A WORKSHEET FOR EACH CREDITOR

Accurate record-keeping will be an essential part of your dealings with the creditors who still give you bad marks. For your reference, use a creditor worksheet containing names, account numbers, credit remarks, and any documents, correspondence, or notes you feel are relevant.

WRITE TO EACH CREDITOR

After studying all the factors concerning each account and reviewing the nature of the credit complaints, write each creditor. Explain your view of how the problem arose. Be specific: give all the relevant details and include full documentation. Be factual, but also appeal to the creditor's sense of good will. Perhaps your company went bankrupt suddenly, or you lost your job. Or perhaps you were detained several weeks in a foreign country while on a business trip, and were unable to pay your accounts on time as a result. Remind the creditor that you did eventually pay, and mention that you did appreciate his services and products in spite of the payment problems that arose. Appeal to the creditor's compassion, and ask him to either remove the bad marks now that the account is settled, or at the very least put in a statement that the account is paid up.

Each of the letters you send should be consistent with the others; if the creditors' new comments show up on your credit file, they must appear reasonable, and should certainly not contradict one another. Use strong, compelling reasons; avoid unconvincing excuses. To help document the process, keep a copy of each letter and receipt with your worksheet file.

ORDER AN UPDATED CREDIT REPORT AFTER 30 DAYS

Allow about 30 days for the creditor to respond to your letter; then order a new credit report to see if the creditor has made any changes in your report. Have the remaining bad marks been deleted? Have some softer marks been added?

SEND YOUR STATEMENT DIRECTLY TO THE BUREAU

If the creditor has not improved the marks on your report, then you should write directly to the bureau and ask them to add your consumer statement to the account in accordance with Section 611(b) of the Fair Credit Reporting Act.

WAIT THE ESTIMATED TIME FOR A REPLY

Now the ball is back in the bureau's court. In a few weeks the bureau should give you a reply. They may also include an updated copy of your report. If your statement appears positive, then you may be ready to start using your credit again.

CONTACT THE CREDITOR BY TELEPHONE

If letters are not working, it is time to use the telephone. This will allow you to interact with the creditor in a more personal way. Before you call, take time to study all the information you have gathered from your credit report, your creditor's responses, and the worksheet you have compiled. Then write a simple outline of all the points that you want to make during your call.

BE PERSISTENT

Sometimes the first call to a creditor will have no effect. Don't be bashful or discouraged. Try again; be persistent. Consider contacting a different person; large companies will have many people working in their customer relations departments. Each person will react differently to you, and sooner or later you will probably come upon someone who will relate more positively to your problem. Once a creditor agrees a change in report is justified, get the person to agree on the phone that he will change your credit status. Offer to send a letter with that agreement in writing, along with a self-addressed, stamped envelope. (Be certain to get the person's name and office address.) Ask your contact to sign the letter and return it to you for your own records. The letter is important; in case he forgets to change your status or later changes his mind about helping you, you can send the letter in an attempt to upgrade your report.

If the creditor will not cooperate with you and you still dispute the negative mark, then the consumer statement is the only remaining tool at your disposal.

TRY AGAIN

If necessary, wait a few months, then repeat the process of protesting negative remarks with the credit bureau. After the lapse of time, the situation may have changed; see what happens when you try the creditor again. After a few months have gone by, you may find a new person in the office who will be more cooperative and willing to help you regain a good credit rating.

HOW TO TURN CURRENT FINANCIAL PROBLEMS INTO A POSITIVE CREDIT RATING

Did you know you can successfully turn even current bad debts into a positive credit rating? Your goal is to approach these creditors and negotiate repayment plans that sincerely demonstrate your ability to make regular payments on time, pay off the debts you owe, and revive interest in you as a customer. In return, you are going to ask you creditor to restore you to a positive credit rating.

How can this be accomplished?

IF YOUR ACCOUNT HAS GONE TO THE COLLECTION AGENCY . . .

If your account has already been sent to the collection agency, try to deal first with the original creditor. A collection agency receives a percentage of what is collected, so they will obviously try to get as much cash as possible from you. The creditor, on the other hand, may have already given up the expectation of full payment. By dealing with the creditor you may have more flexibility to negotiate the time to pay or the amount to pay. Unfortunately, many times the creditor will not deal with the consumer after an account has been turned over to a collection agency because of a contractual agreement with the agency. (Remember, the collection agency is not consumer-oriented, and can be more difficult to negotiate with than the original creditor; it's always best to do what you can to avoid having a debt turned over to a collection agency.)

If you cannot avoid negotiating with the collection agency, however, the following points on how to deal with the creditor can be successfully adapted to a collection agency as well.

MAKE A "WIN-WIN" OFFER TO THE CREDITOR

Your goal is to trade money for a positive credit rating on your credit report. Perhaps you can offer to set up a payment schedule in exchange for a promise to improve your payment history. For example, you could agree to pay 100% of what you owe in twelve monthly installments in exchange for the creditor agreeing to recognize your new bill-paying commitment with better credit ratings.

Again, be specific. Perhaps you can agree that after three months of punctual payments, a negative rating could be raised to a non-rating, and after six months of regular payments, the non-rating could be lifted to a positive rating.

OBTAIN "OPEN ACCOUNT" STATUS

It certainly does not look good if your account is closed for further purchases, and it's especially frustrating to have this problem when you are making regular payments. When you are negotiating an offer with your creditor, ask him to reopen your account while you uphold your end of the agreement. This proposal is more persuasive if you offer to pay 100% of the debt, perhaps with appropriate interest or a service charge added. If the creditor will give you a clean bill of credit health, your extra effort to pay him will certainly be worth it. Just make sure that whatever terms you do finally agree upon are within the range of your budget. You must be able to keep promises made in good faith.

PUT IT IN WRITING

The "win-win" negotiation procedure up to this point can be carried out easily and effectively over the telephone. However, once you have reached a verbal agreement, it is vital to put it in writing. Carefully list all the points of your agreement, reciting them over the phone to get the creditor's verification. Then type the letter, sign it, and send it to the creditor with a stamped, self-addressed envelope. (Before you send the letter, however, you may want your lawyer to check the wording.) Once the creditor signs the agreement and returns it to you, it can become part of your credit record.

HONOR THE AGREEMENT

Now that you have a written agreement, you have only to fulfill it and your credit rating will be restored. So be punctual and responsible; make every payment on time or even ahead of time. If your ability to meet the payment schedule in the agreement should be threatened by unemployment, illness, or a similar serious obstacle, inform the creditor right away, *before* you miss any payments. Discuss your plans for meeting the payments with him and explore ways to solve your temporary setback.

VERIFY YOUR CREDIT UPGRADE

Now that you have an agreement to upgrade your credit, and you have fulfilled your side of the bargain, you should be in good credit shape. But remember to order an updated copy of your credit file to verify that the creditor has honored his side of the agreement and made the promised changes. Allow a reasonable time period from the date he agreed to make the changes; then request your update. If the changes have not been made, you should immediately call the person who made the agreement with you and remind him of his side of the agreement.

If the agreed changes are not made, you could effectively use the process of disputing the information on your credit report using a copy of your signed agreement with the creditor as supporting evidence for the change.

DEALING WITH LONG-TERM NEGATIVES

So far, we have examined how to clear up the majority of problems that can occur in a credit report. However, it's possible that you may have encountered some serious problems such as bankruptcies, court claims, repossessions, or foreclosures in your financial past. These negatives may still "stick" to your credit report after you have tried every method we've discussed. For these major problems the best advice is generous measures of patience and persistence. You will be surprised at how much you can accomplish merely by sticking it out with patience. As these events drift further into your past, they will become less significant in your credit history.

There is more good news on this score: most of this sort of adverse information must be deleted automatically from your file after seven years. So, broadly speaking, you cannot be penalized forever for past mistakes.

One exception to the seven-year stipulation is a bankruptcy, which may be kept on your record up to ten years. And a slightly different set of guidelines comes into play when you request credit or life insurance worth $50,000 or more, or when you apply for a job paying $20,000 or more. The credit bureau may keep an unexpurgated version of your credit history in a separate file that it can only release in the above-mentioned circumstances.

HOW CREDIT CLINICS ERASE BAD CREDIT

Many new entrepreneurs have opened businesses claiming the ability to clear a person's credit record. The chief weapon at the disposal of these businesses is vigorous application of the Fair Credit Reporting Act--a weapon that is, as we've seen, available to you at no charge. Unless you feel it is worth your while to pay someone to follow the steps described in this chapter, a credit clinic is not recommended.

For those who wish to establish a positive credit record, however, the very existence of these businesses is heartening. They are built on the principle we've outlined above, namely, that each item on a record must be proven if it is to remain. Naturally, this is not something you're likely to learn from the credit bureau! Proving these items (whether or not their inclusion in the record is valid) is a troublesome and time-consuming proposition for creditors and bureaus. Very often, the person trying to repair a bad credit rating is the beneficiary. You can make this principle work to your advantage without paying a credit clinic.

BOLSTERING YOUR CREDIT RECORD

Credit reports, as they are originally assembled by the credit bureau, tend to focus on payment problems. But what about all of those positive accounts you have that aren't listed on your credit report?

Do you have sterling payment records that are unmentioned on your record? If so, you can ask to have these placed on the report.

While the law remains unclear about adding favorable items onto a credit report, the Federal Trade Commission has advised credit bureaus that where a report has resulted in unfavorable action against a debtor, the debtor should be able to add to the report to create a more complete and balanced picture of his repayment history. Consequently, most credit bureaus will, for a small fee, contact any creditor you name and add information to your file. The charge will usually run two to three dollars per item.

If you feel adding such information will help in offsetting some negative items on your report, or that it will add perspective to an otherwise incomplete picture, providing current accounts may be well worth the small investment required.

Call non-reporting creditors with whom you have a good relationship. (Remember, your payment record with the organization must be spotless.) Say you need account information listed on your credit report. Once they agree to release your account record, specify which credit bureau will be contacting the organization. Do this for each "good" account you want listed.

Next, you should contact the credit bureau with your list of additions. Ask the bureau to contact these creditors and add the items to your report as soon as the information is verified.

Once you have cleared your credit report of as many negative items as possible and added all your positive items, you should have a new and reasonably good credit report, one that will give you a basis on which to build new credit.

KEY POINTS TO REMEMBER

Good credit is something that must be earned. As you have no doubt noticed by this point, you must work hard to put your right to credit in the best light. Success in repairing your past credit problems depends on your own persistence in using your legal rights to remove negative remarks (by disputing any accounts that you feel inaccurately or incompletely reflect your creditworthiness)--and on your ability to persuade past and present creditors to soften their stances toward you, and cooperate in giving you the credit rating that you now deserve.

Section Two:
SBA Loans

CHAPTER FOUR:
Your Business and the Small Business Administration

The U.S. Small Business Administration is an independent federal agency created by Congress in 1953 to assist, counsel and champion the millions of American small businesses that represent the backbone of this country's competitive free-enterprise economy.

The mission of SBA, simply put, is to help people get into business and to stay in business. To do this, SBA acts as an advocate for small business; at the direction of Congress, the Agency espouses the cause of small business, explains small business's role and contributions to our society and economy, and advocates programs and policies that will help this essential sector. SBA performs this advocacy role in close coordination with other federal agencies, with Congress, and with financial, educational, professional and trade institutions and associations.

SBA also provides new, prospective, and established persons in the small business community with financial assistance, management counseling and training. SBA helps to obtain and direct government procurement contracts for small firms. In addition, SBA makes special efforts to assist women, minorities, the handicapped and veterans to get into and stay in business because such persons have long faced unusual difficulties in the private marketplace.

SBA has about 3,700 permanent employees and more than 100 offices across the nation. To provide quick service, SBA has delegated decision-making authority to its field offices in most of the program areas.

WHAT IS A SMALL BUSINESS?

Broadly speaking, SBA defines a small business as one that is independently owned and operated and is not dominant in its field. To be eligible for SBA loans and other assistance, a business must meet a size standard set by the agency. Specific size standard information is available through any SBA office.

WHO IS ELIGIBLE?

Most small, independent businesses are eligible for SBA assistance. Under the Disaster Loan Recovery Program, owners of both small and large businesses are eligible for SBA Disaster Loan Assistance. So are homeowners, renters and nonprofit organizations.

THE OFFICE OF ADVOCACY

The Office of Advocacy was created in 1976 to be the watchdog for small business within the federal government.

The Chief Counsel for Advocacy is appointed by the President and confirmed by the Senate. Congress created the Office of Advocacy to represent small business interests before other federal agencies and to ensure that small business would continue to be the cornerstone of our free enterprise system.

Under Public Law 94-305, the Office of Advocacy fulfills a number of important functions. It researches the effect of Federal laws, programs, regulations and taxation on small business and makes recommendations to Federal agencies for appropriate adjustments to meet the needs of small business; makes economic evaluations and analyses of the impact on small business of legislative proposals and other public policy issues by conducting research and preparing position reports; and conducts economic studies and statistical research into matters affecting small business. It also evaluates future opportunities, problems and needs of small business. The Office of Advocacy works with the small business community to provide information on small business issues, and assists businesspeople with problems regarding federal laws, regulations and assistance programs. It serves as a conduit through which small business can make policy-related suggestions and criticisms.

The Office of Advocacy has four branches: Interagency Affairs, Economic Research, Information, and State and Local Affairs. These branches are supported by advocates in each of the SBA's ten regions.

In recent years, it has become easier than ever to contact to Office of Advocacy. In October 1982, the Small Business Answer Desk was set up to help callers with questions on how to start and manage a business, where to get financing, and other information needed to operate and expand a business. The Answer Desk can be reached at (800) 368-5855.

The Chief Counsel for Advocacy testifies before Congress and formally comments to agencies on proposed regulations on issues such as liability insurance, employee benefits, health care costs, procurement issues, and pension issues--to name only a few.

The Office of Advocacy also performs both general and specific research. *The President's Report on the State of Small Business* is prepared by the Office of Advocacy annually and contains the most current information on small business performance in the economy. This and other research work determines how small businesses are doing, and what policies and programs are needed to address these issues--data necessary for small business growth and prosperity in the years ahead.

HELPING WOMEN GET INTO BUSINESS

Helping women become successful entrepreneurs is a special--and important--goal of SBA. Women make up more than half of America's population, and currently own over a fourth of its businesses.

Since 1977, SBA has overseen an ongoing nationwide women's business ownership program. In 1983, SBA began organizing a series of business training seminars and workshops for women business owners and for women eager to start their own small firms.

A woman-owned business is defined as a "business that is at least 51 percent owned by a woman or women who also control and operate it."

FINANCIAL ASSISTANCE: REGULAR BUSINESS LOANS

SBA offers a variety of loan programs to eligible small business concerns that cannot borrow on reasonable terms from conventional lenders without government help.

Most of SBA's business loans are made by private lenders and guaranteed by the agency. Guaranteed loans carry a maximum of $500,000, and SBA guarantees of the loan run as high as 90%. Maturity may be up to 25 years. The average size of a guaranteed business loan is $175,000, and the average maturity is about eight years.

SPECIAL LOAN PROGRAMS

In the general area of financial assistance, SBA also offers a variety of special loan programs, including those listed below.

Local Development Company Loans, to groups of local citizens whose aim is to improve the economy in their area. Loan proceeds may be used by the development company to assist specific small businesses for the purpose of plant acquisition, construction, conversion, or expansion, including acquiring land, machinery, and equipment.

Small General Contractor Loans, to assist small construction firms with short-term financing. Loan proceeds can be used to finance residential or commercial construction or rehabilitation of property for sale. Proceeds cannot be used for owning and operating real estate for investment purposes.

Seasonal Line of Credit Guarantees, to provide short-term financing for small firms having a seasonal loan requirement due to seasonal increase in business activity.

Energy Loans, to firms engaged in manufacturing, selling, installing, servicing, or developing specific energy measures.

Handicapped Assistance Loans, to physically handicapped small business owners and private non-profit organizations that employ handicapped persons and operate in their interest.

DISASTER ASSISTANCE

Natural disasters, such as hurricanes, floods, tornadoes, etc., often cause hardship to businesses and individuals. Homes and businesses may be damaged or destroyed. When the President or the Administrator of the SBA declares a specific area to be a disaster area, two types of loans are offered by the agency.

Physical Disaster Loans. These are made to homeowners, renters, businesses (large and small), and non-profit organizations within the disaster area. Loan proceeds may be used to repair or replace damaged or destroyed homes, personal property, and businesses.

Economic Injury Disaster Loans. These are made to small businesses that suffer substantial economic losses because of the disaster. Loan proceeds may be used for working capital and to pay financial obligations that the small business owners could have met had the disaster not occurred.

SBA establishes on-site offices with experienced personnel to help with loan information, processing, and disbursement.

POLLUTION CONTROL FINANCING

SBA assists those small businesses needing long-term, fixed interest financing for planning, design, and installation of pollution control facilities or equipment.

To deliver this program, SBA cooperates with various groups, including state and local regulatory agencies, financial institutions, commercial and investment banks, and other interested parties. Up to $5,000,000 per small business may be obtained through the private markets with a 100% guarantee from SBA.

Who is eligible? Any small business that is now or is likely to be at an operational or financial disadvantage with respect to similar business concerns by virtue of government-mandated planning, design, or installation of pollution control facilities, or at a disadvantage in obtaining financing for such facilities.

Interested small businesses and financial institutions may contact SBA Pollution Control Financing Staff officials in Washington, DC, prior to filing an application. This will provide an opportunity to discuss the requirements of the program.

SURETY BONDS

SBA is committed to making the bonding process accessible to small and emerging contractors who, for whatever reasons, find bonding unavailable to them. SBA is authorized to guarantee to a qualified surety up to 80% of losses incurred under bid, payment, or performance bonds issued to contractors on contracts valued up to $1.25 million. The contracts may be used for construction, supplies, or services provided by either a prime or subcontractor for government or non-government work.

LOAN ADMINISTRATION

After a loan has been made, SBA personnel in district offices service the loan to help assure borrower success in as many cases as possible. In its participation loans, the SBA works with banks in troublesome situations. In the instance of direct loans, SBA personnel work directly with borrowers.

An expanding number of banks today take part in what the SBA calls its Certified Lending Program. Under this program, banks acting under SBA supervision handle much of the necessary paperwork and review client financial status--thereby speeding up loan processing and freeing agency personnel for other assistance to small businesses.

Early in 1983, the SBA began a pilot "Preferred Lenders Program," under which selected banks handle all loan paperwork and loan processing. In 1984, the program was implemented nationwide. There are now over 100 banks in the program. Banks in this program also service the loans. This initiative is in line with the agency's overall efforts to obtain greater private sector involvement in SBA activities; what's more, it significantly trims loan paperwork and processing time.

When loan repayment difficulties develop, SBA attempts to mitigate losses, both to the Government and borrowers, by a variety of means, including Service Corps of Retired Executives (SCORE) counseling and remedial loan adjustments. In the event of business failure, SBA's work may include disposition of the business assets and other collateral security, and/or reliance on the pledge of any guarantors.

SMALL BUSINESS INVESTMENT COMPANIES

Money for "venture" or "risk" investments is often difficult for small businesses to obtain. SBA licenses, regulates, and provides financial assistance to privately owned and operated Small Business Investment Companies (SBICs). Their major function is to make "venture" or "risk" investments--by supplying equity capital, and extending unsecured and not fully collateralized loans to small enterprises that meet their investment criteria. SBICs are privately capitalized and obtain financial leverage from SBA. They are intended to be profit-making corporations. Due to their own economic considerations, most SBICs do not make very small investments.

Primarily, SBICs finance small firms in two ways: with straight loans, and with equity-type investments that give the SBIC actual or potential ownership of a portion of a small business's equity securities. Many SBICs also provide management assistance to the companies they finance.

SBA also licenses a specialized type of SBIC designed to help small businesses owned and managed by socially or economically disadvantaged persons. This type of SBIC is a Section 301(d) SBIC, often referred to as a Minority Enterprise SBIC, or MESBIC.

The administration of the SBIC program is handled by SBA's Central Office in Washington, DC.

MINORITY SMALL BUSINESS

Americans who are members of minority groups, such as blacks, Native Americans, and Hispanics, have long had difficulty entering the nation's economic mainstream. Raising money to open their small businesses has not been easy for them; training, too, has been a common stumbling block. In addition, minority businesspersons have also had trouble finding, keeping, and expanding sales markets.

Members of minority groups who own or who are interested in owning small businesses are, of course, eligible for all applicable SBA programs. But SBA offers special programs to assist members of minority groups who want to start small businesses or expand existing ones. In this effort, SBA has combined its own programs with those of private industry, banks, local communities, and other federal agencies.

Efforts to help minority-owned businesses were expanded in 1978, when Congress approved a capital ownership development program for minorities and placed this effort under the direction of SBA personnel.

The office of Minority Small Business and Capital Ownership Development, located in the Agency's Central Office, is assisted by minority business opportunity field representatives in SBA's regional and district offices. Minority small business staff members cooperate with local business development organizations, and explain to potential minority entrepreneurs how SBA's services and programs can help them become successful business owners.

Under the provisions of the Small Business Act, SBA, working with procurement officials in other agencies, serves as the prime contractor for federal goods and service purchases, and then subcontracts this federal work to small firms owned by socially and economically disadvantaged persons (minority persons, in effect).

SBA is also authorized to place grants, agreements, and contracts with qualified individuals, profit-making firms, state and local governments, educational institutions, Indian tribes, and other non-profit institutions to provide management and technical assistance to eligible SBA clients and small businesses in areas of high unemployment.

BUSINESS DEVELOPMENT

It is commonly agreed that most small business failures are rooted in poor management. In recognition of this problem, SBA places special emphasis on improving the management ability of small business owners and managers.

SBA's Business Development Program is extensive and diversified. It includes free individual counseling, courses, conferences, workshops, problem clinics, and a wide range of publications. Counseling is provided through programs established by SBA's Business Development Staff, as well as through the Service Corps of Retired Executives (SCORE) and its corollary organization of active business men and women, the Active Corps of Executives (ACE). Numerous professional associations also provide counseling assistance.

SBA tries to match the need of a specific business with the expertise available through its counseling programs. In efforts to widen and bolster training and counseling, SBA seeks to involve private sector organizations and institutions in overall management assistance.   Following is a brief summary of what these programs include.

SCORE and ACE help small business executives solve their operating problems through a one-on-one counseling relationship.   Counseling from these organizations, by the way, is not limited to small businesses that have a problem. It is available as well to managers of successful firms who wish to review their objectives and make long-range plans for expansion and diversification.

Small Business Institutes (SBIs) have been organized through SBA on almost 500 university and college campuses as another way to help small business.   At each SBI, senior and graduate students at schools of business administration (as well as their faculty advisors) provide on-site management counseling.   Students are guided by the faculty and SBA management assistance experts, and receive academic credit for their work.

Small Business Development Centers (SBDCs) draw from resources of local, state and federal government programs, as well as from the private sector and university facilities.   SBDCs provide managerial and technical help, research studies, and other types of specialized assistance of value to small business. These centers, which are generally located or headquartered in academic institutions, provide individual counseling in practical training for small business owners.

Business management courses in planning, organization, and control of a business (as distinguished from administration of daily activities) are co-sponsored by SBA in cooperation with educational institutions, chambers of commerce, and trade associations.   Courses generally take place in the evening and last from six to eight weeks.   In addition, conferences covering such subjects as working capital, business forecasting, and marketing are held for established businesses on a regular basis.   SBA conducts pre-business workshops, dealing with such topics as finance, marketing assistance, types of business organization, and business site selection for prospective business owners.   Clinics that focus on particular problems facing small firms in specific industrial categories are held on an as-needed basis.

International trade counseling and training is available to managers of small businesses considering entering the overseas marketplace as well as those desiring to expand current export operations.   Emphasis is placed on the practical application of successful exporting and importing procedures to small business.   SBA works closely with the U.S. Department of Commerce and other government agencies, and with private organizations, to help develop programs to aid small firms in doing business abroad.

Management, marketing, and technical publications issued by SBA on hundreds of topics are available to established and prospective managers of small firms. Those concerned about specific management problems and various aspects of business operations will find these publications extremely helpful. Most are available from SBA free of charge. Others can be obtained for a small fee from the U.S. Government Printing Office. In addition to management assistance publications, brochures describing the agency's programs are available at all SBA offices.

SMALL BUSINESS INNOVATION RESEARCH PROGRAM

The Small Business Innovation Research (SBIR) program began with the enactment of the Small Business Innovation Development Act in 1982. This legislation mandated those agencies of the federal government with the largest research and development budgets to set aside a standardized percent of funds each year for competitive SBIR awards to qualified small business concerns.

In conjunction with this effort, SBA has the legislated authority and responsibility to coordinate and monitor the government-wide activities of the SBIR program, and to submit its findings annually to Congress. SBA maintains a source list of interested small firms and advises them of forthcoming SBIR solicitations to be released by the participating federal agencies.

The SBIR program is authorized through September 30, 1993.

ASSISTANCE TO VETERANS

SBA makes special efforts to help veterans get into business or expand existing veteran-owned small firms. The agency, acting on its own or with the help of veterans organizations, sponsors special business training workshops for veterans. Each SBA office has a veterans affairs specialist to help give veterans special consideration with loans, training, and/or procurement.

For a listing of regional SBA offices, consult the appendix of this book.

CHAPTER FIVE:
About the
SBA Guaranteed
Loan Program

SBA loans have helped thousands of small companies get started, expand, and prosper.

The SBA offers two basic types of business loan. They are summarized below.

Guaranteed loans are made by private lenders (usually banks) and guaranteed up to 90 percent by SBA. Most SBA loans are made under this program. The maximum guarantee percentage of loans exceeding $155,000 is 85 percent. SBA can guarantee up to $500,000 of a private sector loan.

There are three principal parties to an SBA guaranteed loan: SBA, the small business applicant, and the private lender. The lender plays the central role in the loan delivery system. The small business submits the loan application to the lender, who makes the initial review, and, if the loan is approved for submission to SBA, forwards the application and analysis to the local SBA office. If the loan is approved by SBA, the lender closes the loan and disburses the funds.

The guaranteed loan program is the mainstay of the SBA loan program. Over $3.2 billion was loaned in 1987 to over 17,000 successful borrowers. Better than 90% of all SBA loans are financed through the guaranteed loan program. Because it is the one program you are most likely to use, it will be featured prominently in this book.

SBA direct loans have an administrative maximum of $150,000 and are available only to applicants unable to secure an SBA guaranteed loan. Before applying for an SBA direct loan, an applicant must first seek financing from his/her bank of account, and (in cities with populations of over 200,000) from at least one other lender.

Direct loan funds are very limited, and are often available only to certain types of borrowers (e.g., businesses located in high-unemployment areas, or firms owned by low-income individuals, handicapped individuals, Vietnam-era Veterans, or disabled Veterans).

ADVANTAGES OF AN SBA LOAN

There are a number of reasons why so many small business owners and entrepreneurs turn to the SBA for financing.

The major reason, of course, is that these businesses cannot obtain financing through conventional lenders such as banks or venture capital firms. The company may offer too little collateral, be located in an undesirable area, or perhaps be too speculative a venture for the more cautious lenders.

An SBA loan, however, is anything but a "last resort." There are distinct advantages to SBA financing, including the following factors.

Longer Term: Banks and other conventional lenders hesitate to extend business loans beyond three to five years. SBA working capital loans, by contrast, generally have maturities of five to seven years, with 25 year maturities common when financing fixed assets such as expensive equipment or real estate.

Lower Interest: SBA loans, limited to no more than 2.75% over New York prime rates, may offer a borrower lower interest rates than could be obtained without SBA participation.

ELIGIBILITY REQUIREMENTS

More than 99% of U.S. businesses are considered "small businesses" by the SBA. Of the more than 15 million business tax returns filed each year, fewer than 100,000 firms would be considered "large businesses" under SBA guidelines.

For purposes of loan eligibility, a business must be independently owned and operated for profit (except sheltered workshops under the Handicapped Assistance loan program) and not dominant in its field. In addition, the business must meet certain standards of size having to do with the number of employees over the preceding 12 months, or the annual receipts averaged over the prior three year period. Applicants for loans also must agree to comply with SBA regulations mandating that there be no discrimination in employment or services to the public, based on race, color, religion, national origin, sex or marital status.

At present, size eligibility requirements for loans vary by industry and SBA program. For business loans, some general size standard eligibility requirements follow; specific industry classifications are available at your local SBA office.

Manufacturing and Wholesaling. Maximum number of employees may range from 500 to 1,500 depending on the industry in which the applicant is primarily engaged or the nature of the product. The standard is not to exceed 500 employees.

Retailing. Annual sales or receipts may not exceed $3.5 - $13.5 million, depending on the industry.

Services. Annual receipts may not exceed $3.5 to $14.5 million, depending on the industry in which the applicant is primarily engaged.

Construction. General construction: average annual receipts may not exceed $9.5 to $17 million, depending on the industry.

Agriculture. Annual receipts may not exceed $3.5 million.

The process of establishing size standards is a complex one. The basic sources of data used in establishing size standards include the Standard Industrial Classification Manual, which is used as a guide in defining industries. Other statistical sources include the U.S. Bureau of the Census; Department of Commerce economic censuses; the Internal Revenue Service; Dun and Bradstreet; and the SBA's own extensive file of articles, correspondence and information provided by trade associations.

For expert information on the size standard for your industry, contact the Small Business Administration Size Standards Staff, Room 500, 1441 L Street NW, Washington DC 20416. This office develops guidelines and clarifies whether a firm is to be considered a "small business" within a particular industry. It can provide assistance and information about size standards for each industry and quickly tell you whether your business complies.

CLASSIFICATION

A few applicants fail to realize that the success or failure of their application may rest on the classification the SBA assigns to their type of business. You should devote no small amount of attention to this issue. Determine which field or area your product can compete in, state this in your application, and be prepared to back it up. Review the summary of ineligible loan application categories below.

You should be aware of how the SBA formulates its guidelines. A key publication it relies on is the Standard Industrial Classification (SIC) Manual published by the Bureau of the Budget. The SBA also publishes information concerning the nature of companies in businesses similar to yours; reviewing this material is probably a good idea.

INELIGIBLE APPLICATIONS

Because it is a public agency using taxpayer funds, the SBA has an unusual responsibility as a lender. It can decide not to make loans under a number of conditions.   A brief summary of those conditions follows.

Other funds available.   An application may be declared ineligible if funds are available to the business on reasonable terms from sources other than the SBA.   These sources include: private financial institutions; the sale, at fair prices, of assets not needed by the concern in the conduct of its business or not reasonably necessary to its growth; the use of personal credit and/or resources of the owner, partners, management, or principal stockholders; other government agencies that supply credit specifically for the applicant's type of business; and other known sources of credit.

Payouts.   A loan may be denied if the funds requested are for the purpose of paying off creditors who are inadequately secured and in a position to sustain a loss, or if the money will be used for providing funds for distribution or payment to the owner, partners, or shareholders.   In addition, an application may be declared ineligible if the funds are to be used to refund a debt to a small business investment company, or to replace working capital that was used for any of the purposes previously outlined.

Speculation.   The SBA can declare an application ineligible if the loan proceeds will be used in speculation in any type of real or personal property, tangible or intangible.   (It is also forbidden to use SBA funds to free company money for speculation.)

Nonprofit.   An applicant applying as a religious organization or nonprofit enterprise will be declared ineligible.   Exceptions are made for cooperatives that carry on a business activity in order to obtain profits for their members in the operation of their otherwise eligible small business concerns.

Media.   A business such as a newspaper, magazine, or book publishing company or distribution enterprise is not eligible for an SBA loan, though radio, cable, or television broadcasting companies can qualify.

Gambling.   If any of the applicant's or principal's gross income is derived from gambling activities, the SBA will not consider the application eligible. Exceptions are made for concerns with less than one-third of gross income from sales of official state lottery tickets under a state license, or from gambling activities in those states where such activities are legal within the state.

Lending.   If the concern is primarily engaged in lending or investments, this will render an application ineligible.   Also ineligible are otherwise approved concerns using funds to finance investments not related or essential to the enterprise.

Monopoly.   The SBA will consider an application ineligible if the granting of financial aid will encourage monopoly.

Relocation.   If the business is going to use the loan proceeds to relocate for other than sound business purposes, this will render the application ineligible.

Distribution sales.   If the business is a multilevel sales distribution plan, the

SBA will not grant a loan. Typically, such a plan involves sales of soft goods such as cosmetics, household cleaners, or utensils on a door-to-door or house party basis. The profit is often made by recruitment of new distributors.

Government. If the concern's sole proprietor, partner, officer, director, or stockholder (with 10% or more interest), or member of the stockholder's household is a federal government employee with a grade of GS-13 or above, or a major or lieutenant commander (or higher) in the military, an SBA loan application will be declared ineligible. A business is also ineligible if a partner or holder of at least 10% of the stock is a member of Congress, or an employee of the legislative or judicial branch of the government--or if a member of the person's household falls into one of these categories. (Exceptions may be made for the Disaster Loan Program.)

CREDIT REQUIREMENTS

The SBA does impose high credit requirements on the applicant.

A loan applicant must . . .

. . . have adequate credentials and be of good character--a criminal record may scuttle an application.

. . . comply with all federal employment laws.

. . . show that the proposed loan is of such value or so secure as to assure repayment.

. . . show that the past earnings record and future prospects of the firm indicate an ability to repay the loan and other fixed debt (if any) out of company profits, not equity.

It is also worth noting that an existing firm must have enough working capital so that, with an SBA loan, the business can operate on a sound financial basis. Industry standards normally form the basis of comparative analysis.

The SBA prefers to see at least thirty percent of the startup funds invested from the new owner. Minimally acceptable equity ratios vary from industry to industry; however, a 3:1 debt/equity ratio is a reasonable "rule of thumb" for planning purposes.

As noted earlier, the financial assistance you seek must not be obtainable through other resources, such as: a) selling company stocks; b) selling assets owned by you or your company that are not required to facilitate the healthy growth of your company; or c) through utilization of the personal credit resources of you, as owner, your partners, management, or principal shareholders.

Thus, if you have an expensive home or a costly boat, the SBA may frown upon a loan to you. You have substantial assets and collateral--enough to obtain a conventional loan.   Basically, the agency seeks to avoid loaning funds to those who have other available financial resources.

CHARACTER REQUIREMENTS

Particularly when the applicant is opening a new business, the SBA will want to know if he or she is a member in good standing within the community.   The agency will want to see letters of recommendation from friends, business associates, and community leaders, if possible.   A resume is also an excellent way to provide the SBA with a complete picture of you and your company; prepare one and include it in your package.

Complete honesty is required when completing the SBA applications.   While the SBA may overlook certain past problems, a dishonest or misleading answer on an application will probably disqualify the loan automatically.

COLLATERAL

The SBA requires that sufficient assets, to the extent that they are available, be pledged to secure the loan adequately.

Personal guarantees are required from all the principal owners and from the chief executive officer of the business, irrespective of his/her ownership interest. Liens on personal assets of the principals may also be required where business assets are considered insufficient to secure the loan.

One or more of the following may be acceptable security for a loan:

A mortgage on land, home, or building.

Machinery and/or equipment.

Assignment of warehouse receipts for marketable merchandise.

A mortgage on personal property.

Guarantees or personal endorsements; a friend who is able and willing to pay off the loan if you fail.

In some instances, assignment of current receivables.

TERMS OF THE GUARANTEED LOAN

The guaranteed loan program permits the agency to guarantee a maximum of $500,000 and a minimum of $50,000.

Working capital loans are generally limited to fifteen-year terms.   Commercial real estate loans have a maximum maturity of twenty-five years.

Although loans are available for as few as one to two years and as long as twenty-five years (for construction purposes), the vast majority are between five to ten years, with eight years the average.

INTEREST RATES

The SBA sets a maximum allowable interest rate that banks may charge on guaranteed loans. However, the actual terms of your loan are likely to vary. Bank loans guaranteed by the SBA are most commonly made, not on a fixed, but on a variable basis. The variable loans are adjusted in relation to the low New York prime lending rate as published daily in major newspapers. (The prime rate is the lowest rate of interest for banks loans offered to the most creditworthy customers.)

If the loan is for a period of under seven years amortization, the lending institution may not charge over 2.25% above the low New York prime lending rate.

If the loan is for a period of over seven years amortization, then the lending institution may not charge over 2.75% above the low New York prime lending rate. For example, if the prime rate were 10%, the maximum interest rate on a ten-year loan would be 12.75% (10 + 2.75 = 12.75).

The only other fee the lender is permitted to charge is a 2% charge on the guaranteed portion of the loan. For example, on a $100,000 loan guaranteed by the SBA, the guaranteed part of the loan is 90%, or $90,000. Two percent of $90,000 equals $1,800.

There can be no other fees, "points," or prepayment costs added to the loan.

NOTE ON FEES FOR THIRD PARTIES

An applicant for an SBA loan may obtain the assistance of any attorney, accountant, appraiser, loan packaging service, or any other representative to aid in the preparation of the application. The SBA will allow the payment of reasonable fees or other compensation for services performed by consultants engaged to assist you.

For SBA loans, you and your loan packager must sign a form identifying the total cost of the packager's services. Representatives of loan applicants are required to complete Form 159, detailing their compensation for services rendered.

In fact, the SBA requires packagers to specify all services and fees over $300.

A well-prepared loan application, packaged by a professional firm, usually costs between $500 to $1,200 nationwide. If you have a problem with a loan packager, or are quoted a fee above $1,500, talk to your local SBA office.

Before you sign a contract with a loan packager, be certain that all fees and charges have been fully disclosed and are in writing; that you are not being charged on a percentage basis of the loan amount; and that you have a complete list of rates associated with work prepared (ask for the total package fee).

You should also ascertain that there are no required post-loan "management services" contract provisions, or other additional costs based on the amount of the loan, and that you fully understand the scope of services to be provided. Of course, you should obtain a list of references and check them.

Bear in mind that there are no "authorized representatives" of the SBA other than its regular salaried employees. Payment of any fee or gratuity to anyone employed by the SBA is illegal and will subject the parties of such a transaction to prosecution.

If you decide to engage the services of an outside consultant in connection with your loan application, SBA regulations prohibit the consultant or packager from charging any contingency fee or receiving payment except for services actually performed on behalf of the applicant. The amount of the fee must bear a necessary and reasonable relationship to the services actually performed. The SBA can require a consultant to itemize services performed by showing each date, time spent each day, and a description of the services rendered on each day listed. The regulations also prohibit payment of any bonus, brokerage fee or commission in connection with SBA loans.

In line with these regulations, the SBA will not approve placement or finder's fees for the use or attempted use of influence in obtaining or trying to obtain an SBA loan. In the past, many "loan brokers" promised SBA applicants loan approval, exacting their payment by contracting for a percentage of the guaranteed loan. These "brokers" would often demand a sizeable retainer as well. The point bears repeating: absolutely no other fees, aside from the bank's two percent guarantee fee, can be based solely upon a percentage of the approved loan.

Loan applicants having any question concerning the payment of fees, or the reasonableness of fees, should contact the closest SBA field office.

CHAPTER SIX:
How to Apply for an SBA Guaranteed Loan

The process of applying for an SBA loan may appear complicated at first. In actuality, it's no more complicated than the paperwork you would encounter in applying for a conventional bank loan--although some of the information requested may require some detail work.

In this chapter we'll review the proper procedures for completing the various documents that must be submitted to the SBA before your loan request can be considered.

There is an important point to bear in mind before you begin: your application should be completely and thoroughly filled out--preferably neatly printed or typed. Banks and governmental agencies such as the SBA tend to attach greater importance to well-prepared documents than those poorly prepared. There are three main reasons for this. First, such forms ease the burden of those who must process many applications over time. Second, a well-prepared form shows the institution that you are a responsible person who takes the loan process seriously. Finally, a complete and legible application will facilitate processing the loan and help you avoid needless delays in completing your loan.

Preparing a loan request and application for an SBA loan is not difficult. The steps fall into three major categories: collecting the necessary information, preparing the application and forms, and presenting the completed application to your bank.

WHAT YOU SHOULD DO

First, contact the commercial banking officer who handles SBA loans at your bank, and request an SBA loan package. They're available at most participating institutions. Then review the SBA requirements for a loan proposal. These are printed as items one through twenty of the Application for Business Loan (SBA form 4). Familiarize yourself with the requirements as they pertain to your loan request.

Prepare the business plan and financial exhibits. The latter should include a twelve-month income (profit and loss) statement; a twelve-month cash flow forecast; and other relevant financial projections.

Complete the loan applications as required, paying special attention to required signatures and supporting documents. Then, before you actually submit the application, request that a banking officer familiar with SBA procedure review the application and your loan request, so you can attend to any problems or discrepancies that may have escaped your notice.

So much for the actual submission. You will hear in time of the decision on your loan. Bear in mind that if your application is denied by the SBA, you can still ask the bank to make the loan in accordance with the loan guarantee plan. If the bank is interested, ask the loan officer to contact the SBA regarding your loan application. (The SBA usually deals directly with the bank in these instances.)

If the SBA guarantees or participates in your loan, it will require you to complete a number of forms and exhibits, described in detail later in this book.

Note: if you are unable to find a bank willing to participate in the loan, write or visit the nearest SBA office. As noted earlier, the SBA has many field offices. In addition, SBA personnel visit many small cities on a regular basis. (A list of SBA offices and phone numbers is provided in the Appendix.)

PREPARING THE BUSINESS LOAN APPLICATION (SBA FORM 4)

SBA Form 4 (Application For Business Loan) and the exhibits that accompany the form are the heart of your loan application. The information is divided into six sections:

1. Applicant
2. Use of proceeds
3. Summary of collateral
4. Previous government financing
5. Indebtedness
6. Management

Note that a correctly completed Form 4 follows this section.

1. APPLICANT

If your business is incorporated, use the legal corporate name. If the business is unincorporated, use your full legal name. Include the "dba" or assumed business name if this is different from your personal name or the legal corporate name of the business.

Do not use post office box numbers--a street address is required on SBA loans.

If you do not have a federal tax I.D. number for your business, you must request such a number from the Internal Revenue Service, and note on your application that the number has been applied for.

For the "type of business" section, use common classifications such as manufacturing, wholesaling, service, retailing, agriculture, etc. It is also advisable to describe the nature of your product or service; the final classification may read "manufacturer, furniture" or "retail hardware".

Enter the name of the bank--and the specific branch--in which you maintain your business account. Attach a note if the listed bank is different than the bank through which you are applying for your SBA loan.

2. USE OF PROCEEDS

In this portion of the application you should list each of the purposes for which you intend to use the loan proceeds and the amount to be used for each purpose. Inventory, equipment, working capital and other significant items should be listed separately.

Land Acquisition. If you are purchasing land, enter the amount of loan funds that will be used for this purpose. Be fully prepared to substantiate: a) why purchasing land is wiser than leasing; b) why the location you've chosen is better than any other choice.

New Construction/Expansion/Repair. Indicate the amount of loan proceeds earmarked for the cost of construction. Be prepared to describe the construction to be done, and to include at least three bids.

Inventory Purchase. Enter the amount of loan funds you intend to allocate for inventory. You should have already computed a complete cost breakdown of inventory to be purchased prior to the opening of the business. Your opening inventory is what will sustain you through the first few critical months of operation; be certain it is adequate.

Working Capital. Indicate how much of your working capital needs will be supplied from loan funds, and how much will be represented by personal investment in the business. As a minimum, your working capital should not be less than an amount equal to between one and three months' operating expenses. If you have a heavy investment in equipment, land or buildings and must make large monthly payments, for example, you may have a negative cash flow for the first several months, in which case your working capital requirements will be larger.

Payoff SBA Loan. State what amount, if any, of proceeds to be used to pay off an outstanding SBA loan.

Payoff Bank Loan. State what amount, if any, of proceeds to be used to pay off any non-SBA bank loans.

Other Debt Payment. State here any amount of the loan proceeds earmarked for a debt not included in the two preceding items.

All Other. Include here a total of all remaining uses of loan proceeds not accounted for in the preceding boxes.

Total Loan Requested. Add all the preceding figures to get the total loan requested. (Check this figure against your total capital requirements minus the funds you plan to invest in the business. Both amounts should be the same.)

Note: In completing the sections described above, you should be aware that the use of loan funds for personal reasons will invalidate your application. Moreover, the accuracy and reasonableness with which you determine your financial requirements will reflect on your overall management ability and be of considerable importance in the evaluation of your loan application.

Term of Loan. Under the term of loan, bear in mind that five to seven years would be typical for working capital; fifteen years for equipment and machinery; and twenty-five years for commercial real estate. It is essential that the term of the loan you request should yield a monthly payment that you are confident you can safely manage. If you are planning to use the funds for a variety of purposes, then mark the "all other" category, and provide details in a separate schedule as an exhibit to be attached to the loan application.

3. COLLATERAL

The collateral offered to secure the loan (if any) must be listed on the Schedule of Collateral (schedule A). Collateral will be closely reviewed by the SBA and your bank, because the safety of the loan relates directly to the value of the security for the loan. Remember that inventories and accounts receivable have a greatly diminished collateral value when compared with other forms of collateral; this is because they may be dissipated easily.

Collateral for your loan may include one or more of the business or personal assets listed below.

Accounts receivable

Shares of stock or bonds

Inventories

Furniture, fixtures, and equipment

Land and buildings

Personal residence

Chattel mortgage on automobile

Personal endorsements or third-party guarantees

4. PREVIOUS SBA FINANCING

If you or any other principals in your firm have previously received SBA or other government financing, the details of such financing must be referenced.

5. MANAGEMENT

Provide the name of the primary owner or officer of the business, including the individual's address and the percentage share of ownership in the company. Because the SBA maintains statistical records to gauge disbursements to veterans and minorities, it is necessary for you to list any prior military service, as well as your race and sex. Race and sex, however, do not have any bearing on whether your loan under this application will be approved.

6. ASSISTANCE

Anyone assisting, for a fee, in the preparation of the application must complete and sign this section. In addition, such a person must also complete SBA Form 159, "Compensation Agreement for Service in Connection with Application for Loan."

7. CHECKLIST FOR APPLICATION PACKAGE

From page two of SBA Form 4, and continuing to page 3, there are twenty questions, many of which require "yes" or "no" answers. Questions one through fifteen apply to all applicants; questions fourteen through sixteen are addressed to applicants requesting construction loans. Question seventeen concerns those applying for a direct SBA loan, and questions eighteen through twenty apply to those in the export business.

All the questions must be answered by placing a mark in the appropriate "yes" or "no" box, or by following the relevant instructions. (Place a mark in the "no" box if the question does not apply to your loan situation.)

Question one requires that you provide the SBA with a completed SBA Form 912, "Personal History."

Question two requires that you include with your loan application a personal balance sheet as Exhibit B, and advises that SBA Form 413 be used.

Question three requires that you submit as Exhibit C the following items: balance sheet; profit and loss statement; reconciliation of net worth; aging of accounts receivable and payable; earnings projections.

Question four requires that, if you have submitted a brief history of your company, you also indicate, as Exhibit D, the benefits you expect to receive if the SBA approves your loan request.

Question five requires that you provide the SBA with a brief outline, marked as Exhibit E, of the technical education and business background of the persons indicated in the "Management" section of Form 4.

Question six requires that, if there are cosigners and/or guarantors connected with your loan request, you provide their names, addresses, and personal balance sheets as Exhibit F.

Question seven requires that, if you anticipate purchasing equipment or machinery with SBA loan funds, you submit a list itemizing each piece of machinery and its cost as Exhibit G.

Question eight requires that, if you or any of your officers and/or partners were ever associated with a bankruptcy action or an insolvency proceeding, a summary of each action or proceeding be attached as Exhibit H.

Question nine requires that you submit details of any lawsuit in which either you or your business were or are involved, as Exhibit I.

Question ten requires that you provide names and addresses of your family members, or the family members of business associates, who are employed by the SBA, Active Corps of Executives (ACE), or Service Corps of Retired Executives (SCORE). If applicable, you should also indicate the office where such relatives are employed, and attach this information as Exhibit J.

Question eleven requires that you submit information concerning the financial statements of affiliates or subsidiaries, as Exhibit K.

Question twelve requires that, if you either sell to, purchase from, or utilize the products and/or services of any firm in which someone in or connected with your firm has a legal financial interest, you furnish such information as Exhibit L.

Question thirteen requires that, if you presently have a franchise agreement, you attach it as Exhibit M.

Question fourteen, which is applicable to construction loans only, requires that you provide the projected cost of the construction project, along with a statement indicating the source of any additional monies as Exhibit N.

Question fifteen requires that you make certain that all appropriate compliance forms (SBA Form 601) are properly filed. If you are uncertain whether this applies in your case, consult the loan officer at your bank. (These forms, which apply only to certain special case applications, have not been reproduced in this book; however, your bank will be able to provide the applicable forms if necessary.)

Question sixteen requires that you include copies of preliminary specifications and construction plans, as Exhibit O. Final plans will be required prior to the disbursement of funds.

Question seventeen, which is applicable to direct loans only, requires that you attach loan denial letters from two banks stating that your loan request has been denied.

Questions eighteen through twenty, which are applicable to export loans only, require you to check the appropriate "yes" or "no" boxes that reflect your particular business and operational plans.

8. AGREEMENTS AND CERTIFICATIONS

Read this section carefully. It contains binding agreements and certifications that are made by the individual(s) signing the loan application. These agreements and certifications have to do with compliance with appropriate government regulations, particularly those pertaining to discriminatory practices and payments to and employment of certain Federal employees. When executing each form, the signatories are attesting to the fact that any answers and/or statements submitted are true.

U.S. Small Business Administration

Application for Business Loan

Applicant	Full Address
JOHN B. SMITH	10 ELM ST. Anytown, USA 12355

Name of Business: SMITH GROCERY

Tax I.D. No.: 123456789

Full Street Address: 5 Main street

Tel. No. (Inc. A/C): (500)-444-9999

City	County	State	Zip
Anytown	Any	Mo	12356

Number of Employees (Including subsidiaries and affiliates)

Type of Business	Date Business Established
Retail Grocery	1983

At Time of Application **3**

If Loan is Approved **5**

Bank of Business Account and Address: First Bank of Anytown Anytown, U.S.A. 12355

Subsidiaries or Affiliates **—** (Separate from above)

Use of Proceeds: (Enter Gross Dollar Amounts Rounded to Nearest Hundreds)	Loan Requested	SBA USE ONLY
Land Acquisition	-0-	
New Construction/ Expansion/Repair	-0-	
Acquisition and/or Repair of Machinery and Equipment	10,000	
Inventory Purchase	20,000	
Working Capital (Including Accounts Payable)	10,000	
Acquisition of Existing Business	-0-	
Payoff SBA Loan	-0-	
Payoff Bank Loan (Non SBA Associated)	5,000	
Other Debt Payment (Non SBA Associated)	-0-	
All Other Adv + Promo	10,000	
Total Loan Requested	55,000	
Term of Loan	8 years	

Collateral

If your collateral consists of (A) Land and Building, (D) Accounts Receivable and/or (E) Inventory, fill in the appropriate blanks. If you are pledging (B) Machinery and Equipment, (C) Furniture and Fixtures, and/or (F) Other, please provide an itemized list (labeled Exhibit A) that contains serial and identification numbers for all articles that had an original value greater than $500. Include a legal description of Real Estate offered as collateral.

	Present Market Value	Present Loan Balance	SBA Use Only Collateral Valuation
A. Land and Building	$ -0-	$ -0-	$
B. Machinery & Equipment	20 000	5000	
C. Furniture & Fixtures	30 000	-0-	
D. Accounts Receivable	-0-	-0-	
E. Inventory	60 000	-0-	
F. Other	-0-	-0-	
Totals	$ 110,000	$ 5,000	$

PREVIOUS SBA OR OTHER GOVERNMENT FINANCING: If you or any principals or affiliates have ever requested Government Financing, complete the following:

Name of Agency	Original Amount of Loan	Date of Request	Approved or Declined	Balance	Current or Past Due
NONE	$			$	
	$			$	

Complete Small Business Loan Kit/69

INDEBTEDNESS: Furnish the following information on all installment debts, contracts, notes, and mortgages payable. Indicate by an asterisk (*) items to be paid by loan proceeds and reason for paying same (present balance should agree with latest balance sheet submitted).

To Whom Payable	Original Amount	Original Date	Present Balance	Rate of Interest	Maturity Date	Monthly Payment	Security	Current or Past Due
First Bank of Anytown	$ 20000	1/6/85	$ 5000	12%	10/1/89	$ 300	Equip.	Current
	$		$			$		
	$		$			$		
	$		$			$		

MANAGEMENT (Proprietor, partners, officers, directors and all holders of outstanding stock — <u>100% of ownership must be shown</u>). Use separate sheet if necessary.

Name and Social Security Number	Complete Address	% Owned	*Military Service From	*Military Service To	*Race	*Sex
John Smith 000-11-2222	10 Elm St Anytown, USA 12355	80	1960	1964	W	M
Amy Smith 111-00-2222	10 Elm St Anytown, USA 12355	20	—	—	W	F

* This data is collected for statistical purposes only. It has no bearing on the credit decision to approve or decline this application.

ASSISTANCE   List the name(s) and occupation(s) of any who assisted in preparation of this form, other than applicant.

Name and Occupation	Address	Total Fees Paid	Fees Due
NONE	Address		
Name and Occupation	Address	Total Fees Paid	Fees Due

Signature of Preparers if Other Than Applicant

THE FOLLOWING EXHIBITS MUST BE COMPLETED WHERE APPLICABLE. ALL QUESTIONS ANSWERED ARE MADE A PART OF THE APPLICATION.

For Guaranty Loans please provide an original and one copy (Photocopy is Acceptable) of the Application Form, and all Exhibits to the participating lender. For Direct Loans submit one original copy of application and Exhibits to SBA.

Submit SBA Form 1261 (Statements Required by Laws and Executive Orders). This form must be signed and dated by each Proprietor, Partner, Principal or Guarantor.

1. Submit SBA Form 912 (Personal History Statement) for each person e.g. owners, partners, officers, directors, major stockholders, etc.; the instructions are on SBA Form 912.

2. Furnish a signed current personal balance sheet (SBA Form 413 may be used for this purpose) for each stockholder (with 20% or greater ownership), partner, officer, and owner. Social Security number should be included on personal financial statement. Label this Exhibit B.

3. Include the statements listed below: 1, 2, 3 for the last three years; also 1, 2, 3, 4 dated within 90 days of filing the application; and statement 5, if applicable. This is Exhibit C (SBA has Management Aids that help in the preparation of financial statements.) All information must be signed and dated.

1. Balance Sheet   2. Profit and Loss Statement
3. Reconciliation of Net Worth
4. Aging of Accounts Receivable and Payable
5. Earnings projections for at least one year where financial statements for the last three years are unavailable or where requested by District Office.
   (If Profit and Loss Statement is not available, explain why and substitute Federal Income Tax Forms.)

4. Provide a brief history of your company and a paragraph describing the expected benefits it will receive from the loan. Label it Exhibit D.

5. Provide a brief description of the educational, technical and business background for all the people listed under Management. Please mark it Exhibit E.

6. Do you have any co-signers and/or guarantors for this loan? If so, please submit their names, addresses and personal balance sheet(s) as Exhibit F.   *NO*

7. Are you buying machinery or equipment with your loan money? If so, you must include a list of the equipment and cost as quoted by the seller and his name and address. This is Exhibit G.   *N/A*

8. Have you or any officers of your company ever been involved in bankruptcy or insolvency proceedings? If so, please provide the details as Exhibit H. If none, check here: ☐ Yes ☑ No

9. Are you or your business involved in any pending lawsuits? If yes, provide the details as Exhibit I. If none, check here: ☐ Yes ☑ No

10. Do you or your spouse or any member of your household, or anyone who owns, manages, or directs your business or their spouses or members of their households work for the Small Business Administration, Small Business Advisory Council, SCORE or ACE, any Federal Agency, or the participating lender? If so, please provide the name and address of the person and the office where employed. label this Exhibit J. If none, check here: ☐ Yes ☑ No

11. Does your business, its owners or majority stockholders own or have a controlling interest in other businesses? If yes, please provide their names and the relationship with your company along with a current balance sheet and operating statement for each. This should be Exhibit K.   *NO*

12. Do you buy from, sell to, or use the services of any concern in which someone in your company has a significant financial interest? If yes, provide details on a separate sheet of paper labeled Exhibit L.   *NO*

13. If your business is a franchise, include a copy of the franchise agreement and a copy of the FTC disclosure statement supplied to you by the Franchisor. Please include it as Exhibit M.   *NO*

CONSTRUCTION LOANS ONLY

14. Include a separate exhibit (Exhibit N) the estimated cost of the project and a statement of the source of any additional funds.   *N/A*

15. File the necessary compliance document (SBA Form 601).   *N/A*

16. Provide copies of preliminary construction plans and specifications. Include them as Exhibit O. Final plans will be required prior to disbursement.

DIRECT LOANS ONLY

17. Include two bank declination letters with your application. These letters should include the name and telephone number of the persons contacted at the banks, the amount and terms of the loan, the reason for decline and whether or not the bank will participate with SBA. In cities with 200,000 people or less, one letter will be sufficient.   *N/A*

EXPORT LOANS

18. Does your business presently engage in Export Trade?
Check here ☐ Yes ☑ No

19. Do you plan to begin exporting as a result of this loan?
Check here ☐ Yes ☑ No

20. Would you like information on Exporting?
Check here ☐ Yes ☑ No

AGREEMENTS AND CERTIFICATIONS

Agreements of Nonemployment of SBA Personnel: I/We agree that if SBA approves this loan application I/We will not, for at least two years, hire as an employee or consultant anyone that was employed by the SBA during the one year period prior to the disbursement of the loan.

Certification: I/We certify: (a) I/We have not paid anyone connected with the Federal Government for help in getting this loan. I/We also agree to report to the SBA office of the Inspector General, 1441 L Street N.W., Washington, D.C. 20416 any Federal Government employee who offers, in return for any type of compensation, to help get this loan approved.

(b) All information in this application and the Exhibits are true and complete to the best of my/our knowledge and are submitted to SBA so SBA can decide whether to grant a loan or participate with a lending institution in a loan to me/us. I/We agree to pay for or reimburse SBA for the cost of any surveys, title or mortgage examinations, appraisals etc., performed by non-SBA personnel provided I/We have given my/our consent.

I/We understand that I/We need not pay anybody to deal with SBA. I/We have read and understand Form 394 which explains SBA policy on representatives and their fees.

If you make a statement that you know to be false or if you over value a security in order to help obtain a loan under the provisions of the Small Business Act, you can be fined up to $5,000 or be put in jail for up to two years, or both.

If Applicant is a proprietor or general partner, sign below:

By: *John B. Smith*   4/3/89
                                              Date

If Applicant is a Corporation, sign below:

_____

Corporate Name and Seal   Date

_____

By: _____
                  Signature of President

Attested by: _____
                  Signature of Corporate Secretary

SCHEDULE OF COLLATERAL

Exhibit A

Applicant	JOHN B. SMITH		
Street Address	10 Elm Street		
City Anytown	State USA		Zip Code 12355

LIST ALL COLLATERAL TO BE USED AS SECURITY FOR THIS LOAN

Section I—REAL ESTATE

Attach a copy of the deed(s) containing a full legal description of the land and show the location (street address) and city where the deed(s) is recorded. Following the address below, give a brief description of the improvements, such as size, type of construction, use, number of stories, and present condition (use additional sheet if more space is required).

LIST PARCELS OF REAL ESTATE					
Address	Year Acquired	Original Cost	Market Value	Amount of Lien	Name of Lienholder
None					

Description(s):

SECTION II—PERSONAL PROPERTY

All items listed herein must show manufacturer or make, model, year, and serial number. Items with no serial number must be clearly identified (use additional sheet if more space is required).

Description - Show Manufacturer, Model, Serial No	Year Acquired	Original Cost	Market Value	Current Lien Balance	Name of Lienholder
ACE store Fixtures (showcases, counters, etc)	1983	30000	10000	—0—	
(store inventory and accounts Receivable also available as collateral)					

All information contained herein is TRUE and CORRECT to the best of my knowledge. I understand that FALSE statements may result in forfeiture of benefits and possible fine and prosecution by the U.S. Attorney General (Ref. 18 U.S.C. 100).

John B. Smith   Date _4/3/89_

_____   Date _____

PREPARING THE STATEMENT
OF PERSONAL HISTORY
(SBA FORM 912)

A statement of personal history must be filed in triplicate by each party to the loan.   This is the case if:

The business is a sole proprietorship, in which case the owner must file a statement.   A statement must also be filed by the owner's spouse and/or any other person employed to supervise the operation of the business.

The business is a partnership, in which case each partner must file a statement.   A statement must also be filed by each partner's spouse and/or any person employed to supervise the operation of the business.

The business is a corporation or a development company, in which case each officer and director must file a statement.   In addition, each holder of twenty percent or more of the voting stock must file a statement.

Note, too, that any other person not described above who has authority to speak for, enter into obligations on behalf of, or in any manner act for or commit the borrower in the management of business must file a statement.

Because numerous people may need completed statements, this section of the book will take into account the possibility that the person compiling the statements may have to complete more than one form.

PRELIMINARY MATERIAL

You will be asked to supply the name of the company and its proposed address.   Use the relevant home address if a location has not yet been selected. In addition, you will be asked to indicate the loan amount required.   This should agree with the sum on SBA Form 4.   (There is also a section requesting information about the SBA district office and city; the SBA office will complete this.)

1. PERSONAL STATEMENT

List the legal and complete name of the individual whose personal history is provided.   Indicate former or maiden names used, if any, and dates each name was used.

2. DATE OF BIRTH

List the date of birth of the person completing this statement.

3. PLACE OF BIRTH

Indicate birthplace, noting whether the applicant is a U.S. citizen. If not, provide the person's alien registration number.

4. PERCENTAGE OF OWNERSHIP

Indicate the person's percentage of ownership in the company; include his or her Social Security number.

5. PRESENT RESIDENCE

Provide current address information and both home and business telephone numbers, including area code for each. Indicate previous address and the dates resided at that address.

6. INDICTMENT, PAROLE, OR PROBATION

If the person is presently under indictment, parole, or probation, check "yes" here and provide details in a separate exhibit.

7. ARREST OR CRIMINAL OFFENSE RECORD

If the person has ever been officially charged with and/or arrested for any criminal offense besides a minor traffic or motor vehicle-related offense, supply specifics in a separate exhibit. Be completely truthful on this point; a misstatement will generally disqualify the loan, while a minor infraction or one committed well in the past may not impair an application.

8. CONVICTIONS

If the person has ever been convicted of any criminal offense, besides a minor traffic or motor vehicle violation, supply specifics in a separate statement.

9. NAME AND ADDRESS OF PARTICIPATING BANK

Furnish the name and address of the bank that has agreed to participate in the loan. If no bank or lending institution has agreed, note that fact in this space.

WHAT TO DO NEXT

The subject of the statement should sign and date the form using his or her complete legal name and title. Duplicate copies will be used by the SBA to verify the accuracy of the statements.

Review the statement carefully before you submit it. Make sure your statement of personal history is likely to support the request for the loan. Attach any documentation that reflects favorably on the application, including letters of recommendation, resume, and/or lists of special awards or commendations.

United States of America

SMALL BUSINESS ADMINISTRATION

STATEMENT OF PERSONAL HISTORY

Name and Address of Applicant (Firm Name)(Street, City, State and ZIP Code)	SBA District Office and City
SMITH GROGERY 5 main St, Anytown, USA 12356	Amount Applied for: $55000

1. Personal Statement of (State name in full, if no middle name, state (NMN), or if initial only, indicate initial) List all former names used, and dates each name was used. Use separate sheet if necessary.

2. Date of Birth (Month, day and year)
1-1-45

3. Place of Birth (City & State or Foreign Country)
Anytown, USA 12356

U.S. Citizen? ☑ YES ☐ NO
If no, give alien registration number

First: John Middle: Benson Last: Smith

4. Give the percentage of ownership or stock owned or to be owned in the small business concern or the Development Company
80%

Social Security No.
000-11-2222

5. Present residence address:
From: 1965 To: Present Address: 10 Elm St, Anytown, USA 12355

Home Telephone No. (include A/C): (123)-555-9999
Business Telephone No. (include A/C):

Immediate past residence address:
From: 1945 To: 1965 Address: 5 Oak St, Anytown, USA 12355

BE SURE TO ANSWER THE NEXT 3 QUESTIONS CORRECTLY BECAUSE THEY ARE IMPORTANT.

THE FACT THAT YOU HAVE AN ARREST OR CONVICTION RECORD WILL NOT NECESSARILY DISQUALIFY YOU. BUT AN INCORRECT ANSWER WILL PROBABLY CAUSE YOUR APPLICATION TO BE TURNED DOWN.

6. Are you presently under indictment, on parole or probation?
☐ Yes ☑ No   If yes, furnish details in a separate exhibit. List name(s) under which held, if applicable

7. Have you ever been charged with or arrested for any criminal offense other than a minor motor vehicle violation?
☐ Yes ☑ No   If yes, furnish details in a separate exhibit. List name(s) under which charged, if applicable

8. Have you ever been convicted of any criminal offense other than a minor motor vehicle violation?
☐ Yes ☑ No   If yes, furnish details in a separate exhibit. List name(s) under which convicted, if applicable

9. Name and address of participating bank
First Bank of Anytown
Anytown, USA 12355

The information on this form will be used in connection with an investigation of your character. Any information you wish to submit that you feel will expedite this investigation should be set forth

see resume, letters of recommendation (attached)

Signature	Title	Date

United States of America

SMALL BUSINESS ADMINISTRATION

NAME CHECK

Name and Address of Applicant (Firm Name)(Street, City, State and ZIP Code)

SBA District Office and City

Amount Applied for

1. Personal Statement of (State name in full. If no middle name, state (NMN) or if initial only, indicate initial) List all former names used, and dates each name was used Use separate sheet if necessary

First   Middle   Last

2 Date of Birth (Month, day and year)

3 Place of Birth (City & State or Foreign Country)

U.S. Citizen? ☐ YES   ☐ NO
If no, give alien registration number

4. Give the percentage of ownership or stock owned or to be owned in the small business concern or the Development Company

Social Security No

5. Present residence address

From   To: Address

City   State

Home Telephone No (Include A/C)

Business Telephone No (Include A/C)

Immediate past residence address

From   To   Address

BE SURE TO ANSWER THE NEXT 3 QUESTIONS CORRECTLY BECAUSE THEY ARE IMPORTANT.

THE FACT THAT YOU HAVE AN ARREST OR CONVICTION RECORD WILL NOT NECESSARILY DISQUALIFY YOU. BUT AN INCORRECT ANSWER WILL PROBABLY CAUSE YOUR APPLICATION TO BE TURNED DOWN.

6
☐ Yes   ☐ No

7
☐ Yes   ☐ No

8
☐ Yes   ☐ No

9 Name and address of participating bank

The information on this form will be used in connection with an investigation of your character Any information you wish to submit, that you feel will expedite this investigation should be set forth

Whoever makes any statement knowing it to be false, for the purpose of obtaining for himself or for any applicant, any loan, or loan extension by renewal, deferment or otherwise, or for the purpose of obtaining, or influencing SBA toward, anything of value under the Small Business Act, as amended, shall be punished under Section 16(a) of that Act, by a fine of not more than $5000, or by imprisonment for not more than 2 years, or both.

Signature   Title   Date

The Complete Small Business Loan Kit/78

United States of America

SMALL BUSINESS ADMINISTRATION

IDENTIFICATION DIV.

Name and Address of Applicant (Firm Name) (Street, City, State and ZIP Code)

SBA District Office and City

Amount Applied for:

1. Personal Statement of (State name in full. If no middle name, state (NMN), or if initial only, indicate initial) List all former names used, and dates each name was used. Use separate sheet if necessary.

First   Middle   Last

2 Date of Birth (Month, day and year)

3 Place of Birth: (City & State or Foreign Country)

U.S. Citizen? ☐ YES ☐ NO
If no, give alien registration number:

4. Give the percentage of ownership or stock owned or to be owned in the small business concern or the Development Company.

Social Security No.

5 Present residence address:

City   State

From: To: Address:

Home Telephone No. (Include A/C):

Business Telephone No. (Include A/C):

Immediate past residence address:

From: To: Address:

BE SURE TO ANSWER THE NEXT 3 QUESTIONS CORRECTLY BECAUSE THEY ARE IMPORTANT.

THE FACT THAT YOU HAVE AN ARREST OR CONVICTION RECORD WILL NOT NECESSARILY DISQUALIFY YOU. BUT AN INCORRECT ANSWER WILL PROBABLY CAUSE YOUR APPLICATION TO BE TURNED DOWN.

6.

☐ Yes ☐ No

7.

☐ Yes ☐ No

8.

☐ Yes ☐ No

9 Name and address of participating bank

The information on this form will be used in connection with an investigation of your character. Any information you wish to submit, that you feel will expedite this investigation should be set forth.

Whoever makes any statement knowing it to be false, for the purpose of obtaining for himself or for any applicant, any loan, or loan extension by renewal, deferment or otherwise, or for the purpose of obtaining, or influencing SBA toward, anything of value under the Small Business Act, as amended, shall be punished under Section 16(a) of that Act, by a fine of not more than $5000, or by imprisonment for not more than 2 years, or both.

Signature   Title   Date

It is against SBA's policy to provide assistance to persons not of good character and therefore consideration is given to the qualities and personality traits of a person, favorable and unfavorable, relating thereto, including behavior, integrity, candor and disposition toward criminal actions. It is also against SBA's policy to provide assistance not in the best interests of the United States, for example, if there is reason to believe that the effect of such assistance will be to encourage or support, directly or indirectly, activities inimical to the Security of the United States. Anyone concerned with the collection of this information, as to its voluntariness, disclosure or routine uses may contact the FOIA Office, 1441 "L" Street, N.W., and a copy of §6 "Agency Collection of Information" from BOP 40 04 will be provided.

PREPARING THE PERSONAL
FINANCIAL STATEMENT
(SBA FORM 413)

A personal balance sheet must be submitted by each stockholder possessing at least 20 percent ownership, as well as each partner, officer, and owner of the business. SBA Form 413 is necessary for preparation of your personal balance sheet.

The balance sheet must be current (not more than 90 days preceding the date of your application), and it must accurately portray your financial position. The SBA may reject your application if any misrepresentation or inflated entries are discovered.

1. PERSONAL DATA

Enter your name, address, and telephone number as they appear on the Statement of Personal History. If you do not presently own a business, then it is not necessary to list a business name.

2. ASSETS

Itemize the value of all personal assets listed in this column. Write "0" or "none" where applicable. Have your insurance agent ascertain the cash value of any life insurance you own, and enter that value here. Stocks and bonds must be outlined in Section 3, while you must indicate the value of any real estate in Section 4. (An up-to-date real estate appraisal can be obtained from a local real estate agent.)

Continue by indicating your automobile's estimated present value. Use your most recent property tax statements, if applicable, or look up the car's current value in the NADA Blue Book. Then list any other personal property: boats, jewelry, furs, household furniture, appliances, and so on, in a separate schedule.

Indicate the value of any accounts or notes receivable, and/or any mortgage property, if any, and give a detailed description in Section 6. You should also itemize any additional assets in Section 6, and include a separate schedule with the application, if necessary.

Note the total of all these items in the Asset column.

3. LIABILITIES

Be scrupulously honest in listing liabilities. Accuracy can be (and usually is) checked routinely.

Under Accounts Payable, you should list any currently due household bills. Proceed in a similar way through the other categories, noting your notes payable, installment accounts, loans on life insurance, mortgages on real estate, unpaid taxes, and other liabilities. If additional space is required to describe terms of installment notes, then add an exhibit to the financial payments.

Your net worth is calculated by subtracting your total liabilities from your total assets. Therefore, your total liabilities (a negative number) and net worth (a positive number), when combined, should equal your asset column.

(Note: You should make every effort to pay all currently due federal taxes before making application for SBA finances. Delinquent tax obligations may significantly decrease your chances for SBA approval.)

4. TITLES

Section 1: Source of Income. Enter all sources of income from the previous year; refer to your income tax return for this information. Each entry must be detailed in the space provided below this section. Life insurance policies must be available for inspection. With regard to the "Contingent Liabilities" section, list any amount for which you could become responsible for payment at a future date. Complete this part accurately; omitting any unpaid claim, lawsuit, or judgment is fraudulent--even if the claim is disputed.

Section 2: Notes Payable to Banks and Others. Locate your copy of any notes payable and have them available for SBA inspection. Ascertain that all payments are up-to-date prior to filing your application.

Section 3: Stocks and Bonds. Provide the number of shares, name of corporation, and cost price of any owned corporate stock. Call your broker for a market quotation for the date of your financial statement. Enter that figure under "Market Value Quotation/Exchange" and multiply it by the number of shares owned to get the present value. Write this in the "Date/Amount" column. If you own corporate bonds, enter their face value in the same column.

Section 4: Real Estate Owned. Provide complete information concerning any real estate interest you may have. Appraise fair market value if you have not done so within the last five years. Be sure your mortgage payments are current before filing your application.

Section 5: Other Personal Property. This section requires you to list and indicate the value of such other assets as household furniture, jewelry, paintings, stamp and coin collections, boats, or other significant items.

Section 6: Other Assets. Indicate all nonpersonal property of value (such as commissions due, patents, book rights, inheritances, etc.).

Section 7: Unpaid Taxes. Your application should not be filed until you can answer "zero" to this question.

Section 8: Other Liabilities. Name and describe any liabilities not included under the first seven categories.

Section 9: Life Insurance Held. List name of underwriting company, beneficiaries, and face amount.

FINALLY . . .

Check whether you are signing as a primary borrower or as a guarantor. You are a guarantor if your business is incorporated and is the primary borrower.

PERSONAL FINANCIAL STATEMENT

As of _April 4_ 19 89

Complete this form if 1) a sole proprietorship by the proprietor; 2) a partnership by each partner; 3) a corporation by each officer and each stockholder with 20% or more ownership; 4) any other person or entity providing a guaranty on the loan.

Name _John B. Smith_   Residence Phone _(123) - 555-9999_

Residence Address _10 Elm St_

City, State, & Zip _Anytown, USA_   _12355_

Business Name of Applicant/Borrower _Smith Grocery_

ASSETS	(Omit Cents)	LIABILITIES	(Omit Cents)
Cash on hand & in Banks..................$	5500	Accounts Payable.....................$	1500
Savings Accounts........................	2000	Notes Payable (to Bk & Others	
IRA....................................	1500	(Describe in Section 2)..................	-0-
Accounts & Notes Receivable		Installment Account (Auto)	2600
(Describe in Section 6)................	-0-	Mo. Payments $ 205	
Life Insurance—Cash		Installment Account (Other)	3110
Surrender Value Only...................	5600	Mo. Payments $ 312	
Stocks and Bonds		Loans on Life Insurance.................	-0-
(Describe in Section 3)................	-0-	Mortgages on Real Estate................	
Real Estate		(Describe in Section 4).................	30500
(Describe in Section 4)................	85000	Unpaid Taxes	
Automobile—Present Value................	10000	(Describe in Section 7).................	-0-
Other Personal Property.................		Other Liabilities	
(Describe in Section 5)................	5000	(Describe in Section 8).................	-0-
Other Assets			
(Describe in Section 6)................	-0-	Total Liabilities..........................	37,710
		Net Worth..............................	66,890
Total........................$	104600	Total........................$	104,600

Section 1. Source of Income			Contingent Liabilities	
Salary........................$	28000	As Endorser or Co-Maker......................$	-0-
Net Investment Income.............		Legal Claims & Judgments......................	-0-
Real Estate Income................		Provision for Fed Income Tax..................	-0-
Other Income (Describe)*..........	600	Other Special Debt...........................	-0-

Description of Items Listed in Section I _Interest on savings + insurance_

*(Alimony or child support payments need not be disclosed in "Other Income" unless it is desired to have such payments counted toward total income.)

Section 2. Notes Payable to Banks and Others

Name & Address of Noteholder	Original Balance	Current Balance	Payment Amount	Terms (Monthly-etc.)	How Secured or Endorsed—Type of Collateral
First Bank of Anytown,	8000	2600	205	monthly	Car loan
Apex Home Renov. Anytown, USA	3900	3110	312	monthly	Home repair loan (2nd mortgage)

Section 3. Stocks and Bonds: (Use separate sheet if necessary)

No. of Shares	Names of Securities	Cost	Market Value Quotation/Exchange	Date Amount

Section 4. Real Estate Owned. (List each parcel separately. Use supplemental sheets if necessary. Each sheet must be identified as a supplement to this statement and signed).

Address—Type of property	Title is in name of	Date Purchased	Original Cost	Present Value	Mortgage Balance	Amount of Payment	Status of Mortgage
10 Elm St Anytown USA	John + Amy Smith	1965	45000	85000	30500	380/mo	current

Section 5. Other Personal Property. (Describe, and if any is mortgaged, state name and address of mortgage holder and amount of mortgage, terms of payment, and if delinquent, describe delinquency.)

Furniture, jewelry, sports equipment, camping trailer

Section 6. Other Assets, Notes & Accounts Receivable (Describe)

interest in John Smith's Grocery aka Smith's grocery (estimated value = $50,000)

Section 7. Unpaid Taxes. (Describe in detail, as to type, to whom payable, when due, amount, and what, if any, property the tax lien attaches)

None

Section 8. Other Liabilities. (Describe in detail)

None

Section 9. Life Insurance Held (Give face amount of policies—name of company and beneficiaries)

$100,000
Second Union life - Amy Smith beneficiary

SBA/Lender is authorized to make all inquiries deemed necessary to verify the accuracy of the statements made herein and to determine my/our creditworthiness.

(I) or (We) certify the above and the statements contained in the schedules herein are a true and accurate statement of (my) or (our) financial condition as of the date stated herein. This statement is given for the purpose of: (Check one of the following)

☑ Inducing S.B.A. to grant a loan as requested in the application, to the individual or firm whose name appears herein.
☐ Furnishing a statement of (my) or (our) financial condition, pursuant to the terms of the guaranty executed by (me) or (us) at the same time S.B.A. granted a loan to the individual or firm, whose name appears herein.

John B. Smith   4/5/89
_____   _____   _____
Signature   Signature   Date

000 - 11 - 2222
_____   _____
SOCIAL SECURITY NO.   SOCIAL SECURITY NO.

Complete Small Business Loan Kit/84

PREPARING FINANCIAL INFORMATION
ON YOUR BUSINESS

This is one of the most critical parts of your loan application. All financial data must be prepared in accordance with accepted accounting procedures; incomplete or inaccurate financial statements may result in the return of your entire application.

IF YOU ARE APPLYING AS
AN EXISTING BUSINESS

The SBA does not provide specific forms for use in furnishing information in this area; however, participating banks may have ready-to-use forms available for your use. Check at your institution.

The SBA will generally require existing businesses to provide a balance sheet and a profit and loss statement for the last three years (or since the start of the business, whichever period is less). The financial information must be no older than 90 days from the date of the filing application.

The balance sheet and income statements contained in this chapter can be used for these purposes. In addition, the pro forma statements can be used to forecast projected financial performance of the company.

It will also be necessary to reconcile the net worth of the business. Exhibit C of your application is provided for that purpose; however, this same data can be scheduled on your own form.

Accounts receivable and accounts payable must also be aged, using Exhibit C or a separate schedule.

All financial statements must be signed and dated by the owner, a partner, or an officer of the business. If financial statements for prior years are not available, income tax returns for prior years may be substituted in their place.

Never include personal assets or liabilities in the financial statements of your business. Keep your financial information separate from business information.

IF YOU ARE APPLYING
TO BUY A BUSINESS OR
START A NEW BUSINESS

A three-year financial operating plan is normally required of newly acquired or startup ventures, although the SBA may also require existing businesses to submit similar projections.

PREPARING A FINANCIAL FORECAST

Every business--large or small, new or old--needs a financial plan to guide it. Whether you call this an operating plan, a forecast, or a projection, it must show your potential profit or loss and your cash flow over a given period.

Preparing these estimates will probably be the most difficult part of assembling your loan application package. You may want to enlist the services of an accountant. You can use the blank Pro Forma Income statement that follows for this phase.

When you draft your projections--both for profit and cash flow--do them in pencil. It is not unusual to have to recalculate several times.

THE CATEGORIES

Revenue (sales). Total sales include both "cash" and "on- account" sales; net sales are total sales minus returns and refunds. If your business has separate departments, estimate sales for each department separately. Be conservative in estimating sales.

Cost of Sales. Calculate the cost of merchandise sold. If your estimates of sales are by department, your cost of sales will also be by department. Cost of sales should reflect expenses for freight and transportation you pay on incoming merchandise. If employees are paid a sales commission, the commissions should be included in your cost of sales. One method of estimating cost of sales that's helpful if you do not have "hard" figures to work with is to use industry averages. For example, if you know that the cost of sales in a drugstore averages 63%, you could apply that percentage to your sales estimate to arrive at your cost of sales. You can obtain industry averages for your line of business from a number of sources, including trade associations, accountants, or your bank.

Gross Profit. Gross profit (sometimes called "gross margin") is the difference between net sales and cost of sales.

Expenses. Estimating operating expenses involves less guesswork than estimating sales. You begin by estimating each expense individually. If industry averages are available for your line of business, you may want to use them as a benchmark for estimating your expenses. If the sum of your individual estimated expenses is greater than your estimated gross profit, you probably need to reevaluate all expenses and revise some of them downward.

Salary Expense. Base your estimate of salaries on the number of employees you will need, the number of hours they will average each week, and their rates of pay. Overtime must be included if you anticipate high seasonal demands requiring extra hours from your workforce (for instance, before a major holiday). Do not include your own salary draw, if this is listed separately as officer's salary. Include both payroll taxes and other paid benefits you will provide your employees, such as vacation, sick pay, health insurance, etc. A conservative estimate would be 10% for payroll tax, 2% for vacation, 5% for sick pay, and from $100 a month per employee for health insurance.

Supplies. Include all stationery supplies, business cards, and printed forms, as well as pens, pencils, staplers, typewriters, and ribbons; in short, all other items purchased for use in the business (and not intended for resale). Also include postage expenses here.

Repairs and Maintenance. Total all extraneous labor charges for upkeep of the plant/facility. Do not include those normal charges already within the payroll and supplies categories.

Advertising. Consider this item carefully. Identify the kinds of advertising you will require. Will this include television, radio, newspapers, magazines, handbills, direct mail? Estimate the frequency of use and obtain costs based on these estimates. Do not forget special promotions and the separate costs for a grand opening sale. Remember to consider telephone book yellow pages advertising--for some businesses they are quite helpful, though for others they represent a waste of money. Think of how your customer will make a decision to purchase your product, and act accordingly.

Car, Delivery, and Travel. Total estimated company business travel should be estimated here. Try to establish the number and cost of trips, airfare and ground transportation costs, and per diem costs for meals and lodging over the period you are projecting. Estimate gasoline and vehicle maintenance costs; consult your accountant or the IRS for the permissible mileage charge.

Accounting and Legal. Include estimates for accounting/bookkeeping services, incorporating both monthly costs and the amount you will spend to have year-end financial statements and tax returns prepared. You should also add a monthly amount (say $100) to cover occasional consultations with your attorney, as well as initial organizational costs.

Rent. Real estate rent, lease, or mortgage payments can usually be determined accurately--but don't overlook other occupancy costs such as insurance, real estate taxes, or repairs.

Telephone. Account for both local and long distance charges. Your phone company may be able to provide estimates.

Utilities. These estimates include cost of electricity, gas, or oil for heating. In addition, you should incorporate estimates for water, garbage collection, cable television service, and sewer charges wherever applicable. Call the firms or agencies that provide these services and ask for approximate costs of the services you will require. Avoid reliance on old figures that may lead you to underestimate costs.

Insurance. Check with your business insurance broker for a quote on property (including inventory) and liability coverage. Include any special coverage needed for your venture.

Taxes. Local authorities can provide estimates or check recent bills for applicable taxes on your business license, inventory tax, sales tax, excise tax, and personal property tax. Do not include income tax or payroll tax in this category.

Depreciation. For tax purposes, the IRS will allow you to deduct a certain percentage of various fixed assets as a noncash expense. This percentage varies according to the class of assets, and it can change under new tax laws. Call your local IRS office or your accountant for guidelines.

Interest. Be certain to distinguish between your personal and business debts here. Only business debts should be included; do not add the portion of your payment that covers principal repayment. Indicate whether the interest expense reflects interest on the requested SBA loan.

Other Expenses. Outline any other expenses not included in the above categories. For example, membership dues in industry organizations, entertainment costs, or subscriptions to trade publications would come under this category.

Miscellaneous. This category is reserved for small expenditures for which separate accounts would not normally be prepared.

Total Expenses. This is where the sum of all individual expenses is entered.

Net Profit. This is where the amount resulting from the subtraction of total expenses from gross profit is entered.

CASH FLOW PROJECTIONS

When making your projections, you must take into account that sales, profits, and cash are not the same thing.

It is not unusual for a business to encounter shortages of cash even though sales and profits may be high. This is why it is necessary to prepare a separate schedule specifically for cash flow. This projection illustrates total cash inflow and total cash outflow month-by-month over a period of one year. The amounts can be figured fairly easily once you have prepared your projections for sales and expenses.

A cash flow projection is necessary for you to manage receipts and disbursements successfully; with a proper projection, cash is always available to meet expenses as they become due. Projections must address important questions of timing, taking into account the time lag between sales and collection of receivables.

Your accountant should be recruited to prepare a twelve-month cash flow statement. No particular form is required, provided that you include a number of important features.

Cash on Hand. List the sources and amounts of cash you can expect to receive in each of the first twelve months. For a new business, cash will typically be provided through the owners' investment, loans, and sales.

Cash Receipts. These fall into three categories. The first is "Cash Sales": if your "Total Sales" estimate is primarily or exclusively cash sales, enter those monthly figures. (Many small businesses do not permit customers to be billed later for their purchases; accordingly, in these businesses virtually all sales are cash sales.) The second is "Collections From Credit Accounts." Include here the amount you expect to bill your customers on credit accounts. Note that credit card sales (from which 2-5% is usually deducted to cover expenses) are considered cash accounts, and are not incorporated here. The final category is "Loans or Other Cash Injections." This is where you would list, for example, short-term or seasonal loans.

Total Cash Receipts. The sum of the three categories outlined above.

Total Cash Available. The sum of "Cash on Hand" and "Total Cash Receipts."

Cash Paid Out. List all cash paid out each month. Include the payment of monthly expenses, as well as capital purchases--that is, non-expensed (depreciable) expenditures for items such as equipment, buildings, vehicles, and leasehold improvements. Other important categories include: payments on loans and equipment purchases on time payment; startup costs incurred prior to the first month's projection, but paid for after the startup occurs; reserve and/or escrow (i.e., insurance, tax, and equipment escrow to reduce the impact of large periodic payments); and owners' withdrawals for payments such as owner's income tax, social security, health insurance, executive life insurance premiums, and so on.

Total Cash Paid Out. The monthly total of all the items listed under "Cash Paid Out."

Cash Position. "Total Cash Available" minus "Total Cash Paid Out" for any given month. If the disbursements in a month are greater than the income, you will have a negative cash flow. Indicate any negative quantities by putting them in parentheses.

SUMMING UP

Take the time necessary to prepare a reasonable and realistic projection of your month-by-month sales, expenses, profits, and cash flow. Of course, a reasonable and realistic estimate is still an educated guess. The more supporting documents you can supply to bolster your estimates, the better your chance of securing the funding you request. (By the way, the very exercise of putting all the numbers together will make you more knowledgeable about your business, and greatly increase your ultimate chances for success.)

The importance of the forecasts described above can't be understated. They will demonstrate to both you and the lender that you can make a profit from the venture you have decided to undertake; they will prove that you can generate the necessary cash flow to meet your loan payments and other expenses as they become due. The projections are valuable management tools, allowing you to compare actual sales and expenses with those projected for a given month.

If you feel you need more help before you prepare these supporting documents, ask for qualified assistance before approaching the SBA. You may decide to prepare the documents with the help of your local bank manager, loan officer, or SBA loan analyst. Alternatively, you can hire professional help: a competent attorney, accountant, or loan-packaging firm will be able to provide expert aid.

CURRENT INCOME STATEMENT

For _____ (month) and year to date ended _____ , 19_____
($000)

	Current Month		Year to Date	
	Amount	% of Sales	Amount	% of Sales
REVENUE				
Gross Sales	_____		_____	
Less sales returns and allowances	_____		_____	
Net Sales	_____	100	_____	100
Cost of Sales	_____		_____	_____
Beginning inventory	_____	_____	_____	_____
Plus purchases (retailer) or	_____	_____	_____	_____
Plus cost of goods				
manufatured (manufacturer)	_____	_____	_____	_____
Total Goods Available	_____	_____	_____	_____
Less ending inventory	_____	_____	_____	_____
Total Cost of Goods Sold	_____	_____	_____	_____
Gross Profit (Gross Margin)	_____	_____	_____	_____
OPERATING EXPENSES				
Selling				
Salaries and wages	_____	_____	_____	_____
Commissions	_____	_____	_____	_____
Advertising	_____	_____	_____	_____
Depreciation (e.g., on delivery vans)	_____	_____	_____	_____
Others (detail)	_____	_____	_____	_____
Total Selling Expenses	_____	_____	_____	_____
General/Administrative				
Salaries and wages	_____	_____	_____	_____
Employee benefits	_____	_____	_____	_____
Insurance	_____	_____	_____	_____
Depreciation (e.g., on equipment)	_____	_____	_____	_____
Total General/Administrative Expenses	_____	_____	_____	_____
Total Operating Expenses	_____	_____	_____	_____
Other Operating Income	_____	_____	_____	_____
Other Revenue and Expenses	_____	_____	_____	_____
Net Income before Taxes	_____	_____	_____	_____
Taxes on Income	_____	_____	_____	_____
Net Income after Taxes	_____	_____	_____	_____
Extraordinary Gain or Loss	_____	_____	_____	_____
Income tax on extraordinary gain	_____	_____	_____	_____
NET INCOME (NET PROFIT)	_____	_____	_____	_____

ACTUAL BALANCE SHEET

Year Ending _____ , 19 _____

($000)

ASSETS
Current Assets
Cash _____
Accounts receivable_____
    less allowance
    doubtful accounts_____
      Net realizable value _____
Inventory _____
Temporary investment _____
Prepaid expenses _____
    Total Current Assets _____

Long-Term Investments _____

Fixed Assets
Land _____
Buildings _____ at
    cost, less accumulated
    depreciation of _____
    Net book value _____
Equipment _____ at
    cost, less accumulated
    depreciation of _____
    Net book value _____
Furniture/Fixtures _____ at
    cost, less accumulated
    depreciation of _____
    Net book value _____

Total Net Fixed Assets _____

Other Assets _____

TOTAL ASSETS _____

LIABILITIES
Current Liabilities
Accounts payable _____
Short-term notes _____
Current portion
    of long-term notes _____
Interest payable _____
Taxes payable _____
Accrued payroll _____
Total Current Liabilities _____

Equity _____
    Total owner's equity _____
    (proprietorship)

or

(Name's) equity _____
(Name's) equity _____
    (partnership)
    Total Partner's equity _____
Shareholder's equity
    (corporation)
Capital stock _____
Capital paid-in in
    excess of par _____
Retained earnings _____
    Total shareholder's
    equity _____
TOTAL LIABILITIES
    AND EQUITY _____

PRO-FORMA INCOME STATEMENTS

(Four Year Projections)

Item				
Revenues				
Sales allowances				
Net Revenues				
Cost of goods sold				
Gross Margin				
Expenses				
Selling				
Salaries				
Advertising				
Other				
General/Administrative				
Salaries				
Employee benefits				
Professional services				
Rent				
Insurance				
Depreciation				
Amortization				
Office supplies				
Interest				
Utilities				
Bad debt/doubtful accounts				
Other				
TOTAL EXPENSES				
Net Income before Taxes				
Provision for taxes				
Net Income after Taxes				
Prior period adjustments				
Net Increase/(Decrease) to Retained Earnings				

PRO-FORMA BALANCE SHEET

(Four Year Projections)

Item	19 ____	19 ____	19 ____	19 ____
Current Assets				
Cash				
Accounts receivable less allowance for doubtful accounts				
Net accounts receivable				
Notes receivable				
Inventory				
Prepaid expenses				
Other				
Total Current Assets				
Fixed Assets				
Land				
Buildings				
Equipment				
Total Net Fixed Assets				
Other assets				
Total Assets				
Current Liabilities				
Accounts payable				
Notes payable				
Accrued payroll				
Taxes payable				
Other				
Total Current Liabilities				
Long-term liabilities				
Equity				
Withdrawals				
Net equity				
Total Liability & Equity				

PROJECTED CASH FLOW

(Quarterly)

Item	19 _____			
	1st Qtr	2nd Qtr	3rd Qtr	4th Qtr
Receipts				
Cash sales				
Loans				
Other				
Total Receipts				
Disbursements				
Direct materials				
Direct labor				
Equipment				
Salaries				
Rent				
Insurance				
Advertising				
Taxes				
Loan payments				
Other				
Total Disbursements				
Total Cash Flow				
Beginning Balance				
Ending Balance				

CHAPTER SEVEN:
Other SBA Loans

Although guaranteed loans constitute the major part of the SBA's lending program, the agency offers several other loan programs that may be of interest.

SEASONAL LOAN PROGRAM

The SBA can now guarantee Seasonal Line of Credit Loans to finance seasonal increases in the activity of a small business. Loans for retail and wholesale businesses are limited to seasonal inventory purchase needs, while loans for manufacturing businesses are limited to labor and material costs for the seasonal build-up of inventory.

Seasonal Line of Credit Loans can only finance the extraordinary purchase of seasonal inventory--not year-round, ongoing inventory needs.

ELIGIBILITY

The small business must have been in active operation for the 12 calendar months preceding the date of application, and have demonstrated a definite pattern of seasonal activity.   Of course, the business must otherwise meet SBA size and eligibility requirements.

The amount loaned cannot exceed a reasonable estimate of the borrower's current cash requirement to cover labor and/or material costs arising from the seasonal buildup of inventory.

There is no revolving feature in this line of credit. Debt can be built up to the line limit and then repaid closing out the line. In addition, an applicant may have a term loan outstanding at the same time as a seasonal line; however, only one seasonal loan can be outstanding at one time. Each loan must be followed by an out-of-debt period of at least thirty days.

SBA may guarantee up to $500,000 (to be outstanding or committed at any one time) or 90 percent of the line, whichever is less. Interest rate guidelines are essentially the same as for guaranteed loans. The duration of the seasonal line runs from the date of the first disbursement, and cannot exceed twelve months.

You can apply for Seasonal Line of Credit Loans by preparing Form 4 ("Application for Loan"), Form 912 ("Statement of Personal History"), and Form 413 ("Personal Financial Statement"). You will also need to prepare a cash flow projection, as well as current and past financial statements. The cash flow projection should provide for the present payable and fixed obligations, as well as those arising from seasonal activity.

If any portion of the Seasonal Line of Credit will be used for additional employees, the SBA requires that the applicant be current on all payroll taxes, and have in operation a repository plan for the payment of future withholding taxes.

Remember: proceeds from these loans may be used only for labor and material costs for the seasonal buildup of inventory and receivables. Disbursements are made only when there are confirmed invoices for material delivered and/or time records confirming the labor expenses incurred.

ASSISTANCE TO VETERANS

Direct SBA loan funds are available for Vietnam-era and/or disabled veterans. Applications for these funds may be submitted only after all the normal steps associated with applying for an SBA loan have been taken.

You are an eligible veteran if you served for a period of more than 180 days, any part of which was between August 5, 1964 and May 7, 1975, and were discharged other than dishonorably; or if you received a disability discharge.

Upon completing the preliminary steps, submit your loan file to your nearest SBA field office's Veteran's Loan Officer. You will be eligible for a number of benefits.

For instance, the SBA directs particular attention toward providing maximum loan maturity to veterans. Special training assistance and workshops are also available. What's more, your loan request will never be rejected solely due to a lack of collateral, assuming that you or a dependent can supply some form of collateral-- even if that collateral would be considered insufficient by other lenders. In addition, flexible alternatives to regular repayment terms are considered on all loans to eligible veterans.

Under a special appropriation, funds are available for direct loans to disabled and Vietnam-era veterans. (Such loans are made only when financing is not available from other sources on reasonable terms.) Funds from these loans may be used to establish a small business or to assist in the operation or expansion of an existing business. The ceiling on these loans is $150,000.

To be eligible, a veteran must own at least 51 percent of the firm, participate in the actual day-to-day operation of the business, demonstrate an ability to run a business successfully, and show that the loan requested is not otherwise available. There must also be a significant capital investment in the business. Dependents and survivors of veterans are not, as of this writing, eligible for the program.

ASSISTANCE TO THE HANDICAPPED

Special consideration is also given to the loan requests of handicapped persons. Two programs have been created along these lines: HAL-1, relating to handicapped assistance loans to nonprofit organizations; and HAL-2, relating to handicapped assistance loans to prospective small businesses owned (or to be owned) by a handicapped person or persons.

Terms for the repayment of such loans depend on the intended use of the funds and the applicant's probable ability to repay the loan. In those cases where a degree of doubt may exist as to the ability to repay, the outcome shall be decided in the applicant's favor. Fifteen years is the maximum repayment term allowed.

In this setting, three percent per annum is the rate of interest on both direct loans and the SBA portion of a lending institution loan guaranteed by the SBA. The participation loan carries a "legal and reasonable" overall rate of interest. Information regarding the permanent nature of the disability, and the restrictions it imposes on the applicant, must be obtained from a physician, professional counselor, and/or psychiatrist.

BUSINESS LOANS: THE 7A(11) PROGRAM

The primary goal of the 7A(11) program (formerly known as the Economic Opportunity Loan Program) is to provide funds on terms and at maturities that are reasonably affordable to small enterprises situated in high-unemployment areas, or areas with a substantial number of low-income individuals. In addition, the program is designed to provide financial and management assistance to small businesses owned or to be established by low-income individuals.

To qualify for a 7A(11) loan, at least 50 percent of the business must be owned by an individual or individuals whose total annual income, not including public assistance, is inadequate to provide for the essential needs of such individuals. Applicants must also have been deprived of sufficient funding through ordinary lending channels due to social or economic disadvantage.

Firms situated in both urban and rural areas with a proportionately large number of low-income and/or unemployed individuals may be categorized as disadvantaged as well. If the federal government's share of assistance to an individual borrower amounts at any time to more than $100,000 outstanding, a 7A(11) loan may not be approved, guaranteed, or participated in by the government.

Upon giving fair consideration to how the funds will be used and a person's ability to repay, the SBA will schedule repayment predicated upon the earliest reasonable date. Where funds are needed for acquiring realty (and/or various other fixed assets), 15-year repayment terms may be provided. Up to 10 years is allowed on working capital loans.

Unless the applicant refuses to pledge whatever worthwhile collateral is available, eligible applicants will not be refused on the basis of insufficient collateral.

CONTRACT LOAN PROGRAM

The applicant for this program must be a small construction contractor or manufacturing or service industry provider. The eligible applicant must offer a specific product or service under a contract that can be assigned to a different provider (or a subcontractor) if the contractor defaults in performance.

Loans to these applicants are essentially the same as 7A(11) loans, except that the loan proceeds can be used only for the cost of labor and materials necessary to fulfill the contract. These loans are available on a guaranteed basis only, and the standard maximum guarantee rates apply.

The term of these loans is twelve months from the date of the first disbursement (except in the case of large contracts, in which case an eighteen-month maturity can be approved). The interest rate is held at a maximum of the current prime rate plus 2.25%, with a possible additional servicing fee of 2% being charged when justified. The applicant must have been in business for a minimum of one year.

LOCAL DEVELOPMENT COMPANY (502) LOANS

The purpose of these loans is to facilitate plant acquisition, construction, conversion, and expansion (including land, fixed machinery, and equipment). Approval is contingent upon the applicant's ability to certify that the project will result in a significant positive impact on the community. This positive impact may come about as the result of diversification or stabilization of the economy within the neighborhood, job development, or the achievement of a national objective.

The loan is available on a guaranteed basis only, with a maximum guarantee of $500,000. The interest rate is the same as the 7A(11) guaranteed loan, but there is a 1% fee on the guaranteed portion of the loan. The term can extend as long as 25 years, plus the necessary project construction time. The loan must be reasonably secured so as to assure repayment. The development company or small business concern must furnish 10% of the project cost.

CERTIFIED DEVELOPMENT COMPANY (504) LOANS

Eligibility requirements here are the same as for 502 loans, as is the general purpose behind the loan. These loans, however, are granted to development companies on the basis of a requirement that they provide expansion or retention of employment equal to one person for each $15,000 of the loan amount. Funding is accomplished through the sale of SBA-guaranteed debentures; the interest rate is determined at the time of the sale of these debentures. The loan term is ten to twenty years. The development company must furnish 10% of the project cost, but it can combine forces with conventional first mortgage financing to enable large projects to be undertaken.

ENERGY LOANS

With regard to these loans, applicants must, generally speaking, be in the business of manufacturing, selling, installing, servicing, or developing specific energy measures and/or products. Basically, the same criteria that apply for a 7(A) loan apply here. However, there is greater risk inherent in granting these loans than in others; the SBA, accordingly, places more emphasis on the technical soundness of the product or process, and in the technical qualifications of the applicant.

EXPORT LINE OF CREDIT

The purpose of this program is to help small businesses export their products and services abroad. Eligibility requirements area the same as for 7A(11) business loans. Loan proceeds must be used to finance labor and materials needed for manufacturing or wholesaling for export and/or to penetrate or develop foreign markets. Examples of expenses that would fall into these categories include: professional export marketing advice or services; foreign business travel; participation in trade shows.

These loans are available on a guaranteed basis only, and maximum guarantee limits apply. The term may not exceed eighteen months. The interest rate is held at a maximum of the current prime rate plus 2.25%, with a possible additional servicing fee of up to 2% when such a charge is deemed justified.

Section Three: Bank Loans

CHAPTER EIGHT:
The Basics of Borrowing from Banks

SOUND FOOTING

It's been estimated that more businesses fail because of improperly structured financing than any other factor. Improper financing can restrict growth, create adverse tax consequences and needlessly increase personal liability. The future of your business is influenced (if not determined outright) by how you finance your venture. In this chapter, we'll examine the challenges of borrowing from commercial banks--and review some essentials (many of which are covered in greater detail elsewhere in this book) that must precede your application.

Once you consider financing (as you must when you approach a commercial bank for a loan), you face a maze of questions:

How much capital do I really need?

How should capital requirements be divided between borrowed funds and invested funds?

What are the best financing sources for the loan I need?

How do I successfully apply for business loans?

What financing terms should be negotiated?

How should the loan be structured?

ESTIMATING YOUR FINANCING NEEDS

To determine your financing needs, it's necessary to go beyond calculating the amount required to buy or start your business. You must also accurately forecast the capital needed to operate and build the new enterprise once it is underway.

Many borrowers make the error of viewing financing as a two-step process. They first exhaust their borrowing power to finance the acquisition, and later attempt to find the additional financing necessary to properly operate or expand the business.

Such short-sighted financing efforts are almost always unsuccessful; the available collateral has usually been exhausted by the time the second stage begins. It is rarely feasible to restructure the original financing arrangements to allow additional financing.

When projecting your financing requirements, you must consider capital needed to:

Build sufficient inventory to achieve sales projected under the business forecast.

Renovate and modernize the business.

Add or replace fixtures and equipment.

Finance accounts receivable.

Finance planned advertising or promotional programs.

Maintain adequate working capital.

You'll need to use both operational plans and financial forecasts for the business as guides. It makes little sense to acquire a struggling business on the premise of your ability to make operational changes, without the financial resources necessary to achieve those changes!

Do not forget to check items that can affect cash flow and working capital needs. Examine the balance sheet; redeploying assets and liabilities can often release cash, thereby reducing the need for financing. Similarly, your inventory may be excessive; if so, you might consider partial liquidation in order to raise cash. When buying an existing business, you must take into account the implications of the purchase of the seller's receivables. These can have a dramatic effect on your financing needs; purchasing accounts receivable provides an immediate income stream. On the other hand, if you must begin by generating your own receivables, cash flow will be significantly reduced during the startup period.

You must ask yourself another important question before you decide how much money you need: what idle assets can be disposed of for cash? Each cash-flow factor should be carefully considered by you and your accountant, for purposes of accurately projecting financing needs.

FINDING THE MONEY

When financing for a small business acquisition, you should consider three primary sources:

1. Internal Financing: This includes seller financing, assumption of debt, and similar financing opportunities existing within the business and made available to the buyer under an acquisition.

2. External Financing: This includes funds borrowed from external sources, such as banks, SBIC's and other third party lenders.

3. Equity: This is the amount invested from your own funds and not scheduled for repayment.

Bank financing is the most frequently used source for business loans; accordingly, it's a good idea to take a close look now at how banks work.

MISUNDERSTOOD PLAYERS

Even though you can find them virtually anywhere, banks still remain the most misunderstood and intimidating players in the commercial world.

Why the mystery? After all, it's a rare person who hasn't dealt with a bank. Certainly the average applicant for a business loan has a checking account, and probably a savings account or two, as well. We often forget, however, that we are the bank's customers, and that they depend on us for business.

Consider that your bank pays you eight percent for the use of your money, and lends it to someone else for thirteen percent. How do you think banks pay for those fancy buildings?

On the other hand, many assume that obtaining a loan for a business venture is easier than it is. This misperception is usually rooted in experience with loans for purposes other than running a business. People think of what it takes to put together a loan for a new car, or a twenty-year mortgage on a home. You walk in, fill out an application, wait a few days for a quick credit check--then the check comes in the mail. A business loan, however, is considerably more complicated. To be successful in obtaining a business loan from a bank, far more is required than simply knowing how to complete an application.

There are a number of unfortunate myths about banks. One is that the bank's purpose is to loan money. Actually, money is only the inventory. A bank is in the business of making money. Profitable loans are what banks are after!

Another myth is that an entrepreneur can apply to a bank for a "standard business loan." There's no such thing as a standard loan. Banks can and will undertake to negotiate individual loan terms, depending on your persuasiveness and the strength of your deal.

Then there is the myth of the bank as guardian of the public trust. Banks are in fact institutions operated for profit, and you can face stiff competition for the bank's dollars. After all, a bank only has a certain amount of money; the number of dollars a bank has to lend depends on its own performance and on economic conditions. Loan officers, like most businesspeople, are under pressure to make profitable decisions. Even in the best of times, competition for financing can be keen. To win financing you must convince a bank you will have both the profits and security for the loan to make financing justifiable.

Finally, it's important to note that the relationship between banker and customer is much more of a partnership than commonly believed. Assuming your proposals are sensible ones, banks need you as much as you need them. Without people willing to pay interest, a bank isn't much of a bank.

With the proper perspective and a solid business plan, you can gain the competitive edge in obtaining necessary financing for your business. As in any business deal, a winning attitude is essential. Remember, at today's interest rates you are not asking for favors; you are initiating a business relationship, and there's no reason to be shy or intimidated as you do so.

THE ADVANTAGES OF BANK FINANCING

The advantages of borrowing from a bank are:

Banks are used to dealing with businesses, and can supply financing plans that are comparatively affordable and well-suited to your needs.

Banks can give you expert advice about businesses related to yours-- businesses they deal with regularly.

Borrowing from a bank is better for your credit standing than borrowing from other sources (such as government agencies).

Banks offer a wide variety of loan packages and can be quite flexible.

Banks offer many important business services you may decide to take advantage of, including: credit references on customers or potential customers; financial, investment and estate advisory services; discounting customer accounts and notes payable; check certification; safe deposit boxes; night depositories; and collections of remittances.

DISADVANTAGES OF BANK FINANCING

Several disadvantages of banks include:

Their conservative approach when considering loans. Banks are about the most difficult loan sources.

The technical requirements (financial spreadsheets, projected budgets) of presenting a loan. Usually, banks want to see more information (and more precise information) than other sources.

Their ongoing role as "monitor" of their investment. Though banks are regulated by the federal government, they are still out to make money, just like all other businesses. Accordingly, they have to be careful their loans don't fail--even after they make a decision to lend money. The bank will probably watch your business closely, and evaluate your progress toward goals.

KNOCKING ON THE RIGHT DOORS

Knowing which banks to ask for money can be half the battle. No two banks are alike; neither are any two bankers. You have to find not only the best bank for you, but also the banker within the bank who has both the authority and willingness to grant your loan.

Banks, like most other businesses, have their own specialties or market niches. Do the "homework" necessary to learn what types of loan a given bank specializes in, then narrow your sights to the right bank.

The right bank for your business is probably not the bank you got your home mortgage from. Business loans are best obtained at commercial banks, while home mortgages and consumer loans are typically in the domain of savings banks, cooperatives, and credit unions.

If you're in the market for a loan under $100,000, concentrate primarily on small banks. Matching the size of the bank to your loan is important. To a large metropolitan bank, you're likely to be considered nothing more than a small fish in a big pond. How important can you be to the big banks when their customers frequently deal in $10 million transactions?

Stay close to home. Banks may have legal restrictions or internal policies against lending to businesses beyond a given geographic area, and usually prefer to be close to their customers.

Remember that banks are more than brick and stone. They're operated by people, and people have likes and dislikes, prejudices and preferences. For instance, several years ago a woman's group chartered a local bank exclusively for the purpose of lending to female entrepreneurs, and today the bank is reportedly doing a landslide business. No two banks are identical; what one bank will turn down another may accept with unbridled enthusiasm.

HOW TO CHOOSE

What should you look for in choosing a bank? There are five main points to consider.

1. Is the banker progressive? Has he kept pace with changing conditions, and is he alert to the developing requirements of the community?

2. Does the management of the bank combine integrity, experience, ability and initiative?

3. How does the banker approach your problems? Does he appear interested and helpful? These are questions you can answer only by having a conference with the banker directly. Be straightforward in any interview you arrange. Don't hold back.

4. Can you obtain the credit you need? Be sure the banker understands your particular needs and is willing and able to service them.

5. How large is the bank? Generally speaking, size should probably not be the deciding factor in choosing a bank. It may make a difference, however, in the types and amount of credit available, the services offered, the prestige your initiative requires, and so on. Sometimes small banks are the best bet because they might be more liberal and offer more personal service. On the other hand, if you can justify a need for special services, large amounts of credit, or international services, a larger bank is preferable.

Although most small businesspeople don't interview bankers before establishing bank relationships, interviewing and carefully selecting your bank can be one of the most important undertakings of your business.

WHAT TYPE OF LOAN DO YOU NEED?

There are many types of loans; it's important to understand precisely the type of financing that will best serve your needs.

Short-Term Loans. Short-term loans are designed to help meet the daily operational needs of the business: salaries, rent, insurance, advertising, payment of suppliers, etc. These loans are a principal type of bank lending. Such loans are written for a short duration (30, 60, or 90 days) and are based upon the operating or business cycle of the individual firm. Operating loans vary in length of maturity since they are adapted to specific business patterns. Many short-term loans are "revolving loans": the loan proceeds are used to purchase inventory, pay for manufacturing or processing expenses, or for market and delivery costs, and the loan is repaid when the business completes this process and collects. When new sales generate new accounts receivable, new revolving loans are initiated. Short-term loans are ordinarily easier to get than intermediate and long-term loans, especially for the small businessperson. They are often unsecured and may require lower interest rates than longer-term loans.

Intermediate-Term Loans. An intermediate-term loan (or term loan) provides you with capital for other than temporary needs. For example, you may need new equipment to increase your output, but lack the cash to pay for it. With an intermediate term loan, you can acquire title to the machine immediately. During the life of the loan, the equipment will be helping to produce income from which you can pay the installments and interest. Intermediate-term loans are commonly used to purchase existing businesses, to help establish new ones, to provide additional working capital, and to replace long-term indebtedness that carries a higher rate of interest. They may be either secured or unsecured. Payment may be made monthly, quarterly, semiannually or annually.

Accounts-Receivable Loans. Accounts-receivable financing can be used as a basis for short- or intermediate-term loans from your bank. If your working capital is limited or your sales volume fluctuates, you will find this type of financing particularly useful. When you obtain an accounts-receivable loan, you pledge or assign all or part of your accounts receivable as security for the loan. The agreement for the loan specifies what the percentage of the volume of receivables you assign will be loaned to you. In the case of the bank loan, this will usually be from 75 to 80 percent of sound receivables. The agreement also sets forth your rights and liabilities, those of the lender, the conditions under which each assignment is to operate, and the charges, which may include both interest and service charges.

Inventory Loans. Inventory financing is often necessary when large amounts of inventory are tied up for a period of time. Some firms, especially those in manufacturing, have long cycles for purchasing, production and warehousing, which would make inventory financing important. With inventory loans the bank does not take physical possession of the inventory. The bank may have a lien on, or title to, the goods stored separately on the premises or in a storage warehouse. Inventory that would not be held this way includes small quantities of goods, fast moving items, and work in process. In floor financing the dealer has possession of the merchandise, but title to it remains with a bank or other lender.

Fixed Asset Loans. Fixed asset financing involves financing large capital items (improvements, land and buildings, equipment and fixtures) and is for the longest term of the types of financing. In most cases loans secured by fixed assets are for a term in excess of one year. When you are purchasing equipment and using it as collateral, that is, making a down payment on the equipment and borrowing the rest from the bank, the bank takes a chattel mortgage. The chattel transfers ownership (title) to the bank while the borrower uses the equipment.

(Note: one type of long-term loan is the Small Business Administration 90-percent-guaranteed loan through a bank, discussed elsewhere in this book. Its term is from five to fifteen years; it can be used for equipment, real estate, improvements, and working capital.)

HOW TO WIN FINANCING

Picture yourself sitting across the bank president's desk. You announce that you need only $60,000 to buy a restaurant, one that you know is "bound to hit big; real big." You explain excitedly what a great deal it is, how much money you're going to make, and how you intend to buy the facility. Despite your enthusiasm, the banker abruptly calls the meeting to a conclusion, and politely shows you the door--without the cash. Where did you go wrong?

The answer is simple. You acted like an amateur, and banks rarely lend money to amateurs. To be sure, if you happen to have a multi-million dollar net worth, the bank may conveniently overlook problems and focus instead on your considerable assets. But if you are going into business on little more than hope, you must think professionally, and that means approaching financing professionally. In short, you must know precisely what the bank will look for. These are referred to as the three C's of loanmanship.

Character: How do you come across in person? Are you trustworthy? Do you have a history of good credit?

Cash Flow: Does the business offer sufficient cash flow and profit after expenses to pay back the loan? Your best intentions mean little if you can't prove that the numbers work and that you have the capacity to pay.

Collateral: What does the bank risk? Should your loan go into default, will the bank have sufficient collateral to recover the balance owed?

Successful borrowers know banks view loan applications based largely on these three points; accordingly, they highlight them in a clear, logical and businesslike proposal.   Follow the checklist below, and you can draft your own professional loan proposal.   (Note: see also the separate section of this book on preparing your business plan.)

1. Credit and Personal History [Character]:

Name and address

Family status

Employment history

Experiences in related business

Education

Personal liabilities

Military status

Bank references

Credit references

2.   Financial Information on the Business [Cash Flow]:

Brief description of business

Brief history of business

Tax returns for two years

Projected cash flow statement for loan period

Summary of proposed business changes

Lease or proposed lease terms

3.   Collateral:

Business Assets

Acquisition cost or replacement cost

Liquidation value of assets

4. Proposed Loan:

Amount required

Loan period

Interest terms

Identification of guarantors

Collateral to be pledged

A financing request containing these points provides the banker with everything necessary to evaluate your loan properly. You make the banker's job far easier by anticipating crucial questions. Your banker knows he's dealing with a professional, which allows him to place a measure of confidence in your proposals. Justify that confidence by having your accountant join you in your negotiations at the bank. Bankers feel more comfortable when they know an accountant is helping to navigate your venture.

A final word of caution: be absolutely certain your numbers support your loan request. If your loan demands payments of $2,000 per month, you will fail in your loan request if your cash flow statement reveals only $1,000 in available income. Be prepared to defend your proposal vigorously; your banker is likely to ask many probing questions.

NEGOTIATING THE MOST ADVANTAGEOUS LOAN TERMS

Once a bank looks favorably upon your loan request, there are several rules of thumb you can follow to help save money.

Negotiate interest rates. Like other business deals, interest rates on loans are subject to hard bargaining. Banks will often drop the interest rate by a point or two if your business plan is strong.

Try to secure the longest possible loan. Long-term loans lower monthly payments and help you conserve cash flow.

Never borrow personally. Your corporation, not you, should borrow the money. If you borrow as an individual, the bank cannot claim the proceeds of the business assets in the event of default, and you then will have to repay the loan personally. Ask your attorney to help structure the loan to provide you maximum personal protection.

If at all possible, pledge only business assets as collateral. Protect your personal assets; don't risk your own property, no matter how "certain" you are that a default will never occur. Business assets may be enough to keep the bank from going after your personal assets, but why take the chance?

Never falsify your loan application. False statements can cause you big headaches, including immediate foreclosure and non-discharge of the bank debt should you later declare bankruptcy.

Never settle for the first loan offer. Remember, banks can be found on every corner. Shop around. You may land a better deal at the bank next door.

WHEN THE BANK SAYS "NO"

Don't let failure discourage you. You may wander from bank to bank failing each and every time, but if you're wise you'll want to find out why. Once you detect the flaw in your proposal you can correct it.

Rejection can actually be beneficial. It can pinpoint a weakness in your loan proposal or a fatal flaw in your business idea.

Don't accept a loan rejection and simply stroll on to the next bank. First find out why the loan was declined. Some banks hedge on candid answers because they neither want to offend or engage in long conversation. But push for an honest answer. Plenty of loan rejections have saved borrowers a bundle on their faulty ideas. Sometimes it takes experienced advice from a banker to set you straight.

Don't look on your banker as an adversary, but as an ally in evaluating the soundness of your plans. Your banker may see weaknesses you overlooked or raise important questions. Listen closely. If your banker raises some doubts in your own mind then investigate further until you are satisfied. Still, you must eventually follow your own entrepreneurial instincts. Thousands of success stories have thumbed their noses at bankers who said "no".

Banks sometimes say "no" when they really mean "yes," but to a different loan arrangement. Perhaps you have been rejected for a $100,000 loan. Is the bank willing to loan $75,000? Perhaps your request for interest at 11 percent was below their current rate of 13 percent. Possibly more collateral would do the trick. Few deals are so fundamentally weak that they fail to qualify for any loan whatsoever. Try to obtain a financing counteroffer that can still satisfy your needs and help you meet your objectives.

Appendix

SBA DOCUMENTS

Note: forms may be photocopied by the purchaser for his or her own use; all other reproduction, including reproduction for resale, is prohibited.

SMALL BUSINESS ADMINISTRATION

POLICY AND REGULATIONS CONCERNING REPRESENTATIVES AND THEIR FEES

An applicant for a loan from SBA may obtain the assistance of any attorney, accountant, engineer, appraiser or other representative to aid him in the preparation and presentation of his application to SBA; however, such representation is not mandatory. In the event a loan is approved, the services of an attorney may be necessary to assist in the preparation of closing documents, title abstracts, etc. SBA will allow the payment of reasonable fees or other compensation for services performed by such representatives on behalf of the applicant.

There are no "authorized representatives" of SBA, other than our regular salaried employees. Payment of any fee or gratuity to SBA employees is illegal and will subject the parties to such a transaction to prosecution.

SBA Regulations (Part 103, Sec. 103.13-5(c)) prohibit representatives from charging or proposing to charge any contingent fee for any services performed in connection with an SBA loan unless the amount of such fee bears a necessary and reasonable relationship to the services actually performed; or to charge any fee which is deemed by SBA to be unreasonable for the services actually performed; or to charge for any expenses whch are not deemed by SBA to have been necessary in connection with the application. The Regulations (Part 122, Sec. 122.19) also prohibit the payment of any bonus, brokerage fee or commission in connection with SBA loans.

In line with these Regulations SBA will not approve placement or finder's fees for the use or attempted use of influence in obtaining or trying to obtain an SBA loan, or fees based solely upon a percentage of the approved loan or any part thereof.

Fees which will be approved will be limited to reasonable sums for services actually rendered in connection with the application or the closing, based upon the time and effort required, the qualifications of the representative and the nature and extent of the services rendered by such representative. Representatives of loan applicants will be required to execute an agreement as to their compensation for services rendered in connection with said loan.

It is the responsibility of the applicant to set forth in the appropriate section of the application the names of all persons or firms engaged by or on behalf of the applicant. Applicants are required to advise the Regional Office in writing of the names and fees of any representatives engaged by the applicant subsequent to the filing of the application. This reporting requirement is approved under OMB Approval Number 3245-0016.

Any loan applicant having any question concerning the payment of fees, or the reasonableness of fees, should communicate with the Field Office where the application is filed.

Application for Business Loan

Applicant	Full Address	

Name of Business		Tax I.D. No.
Full Street Address		Tel. No. (Inc. A/C)
City	County	State	Zip	Number of Employees (Including subsidiaries and affiliates)
Type of Business		Date Business Established	At Time of Application _____
Bank of Business Account and Address		If Loan is Approved _____
		Subsidiaries or Affiliates _____ (Separate from above)

Use of Proceeds: (Enter Gross Dollar Amounts Rounded to Nearest Hundreds)	Loan Requested	SBA USE ONLY
Land Acquisition		
New Construction/ Expansion/Repair		
Acquisition and/or Repair of Machinery and Equipment		
Inventory Purchase		
Working Capital (Including Accounts Payable)		
Acquisition of Existing Business		
Payoff SBA Loan		
Payoff Bank Loan (Non SBA Associated)		
Other Debt Payment (Non SBA Associated)		
All Other		
Total Loan Requested		
Term of Loan		

Collateral

If your collateral consists of (A) Land and Building, (D) Accounts Receivable and/or (E) Inventory, fill in the appropriate blanks. If you are pledging (B) Machinery and Equipment, (C) Furniture and Fixtures, and/or (F) Other, please provide an itemized list (labeled Exhibit A) that contains serial and identification numbers for all articles that had an original value greater than $500. Include a legal description of Real Estate offered as collateral.

	Present Market Value	Present Loan Balance	SBA Use Only Collateral Valuation
A. Land and Building	$	$	$
B. Machinery & Equipment			
C. Furniture & Fixtures			
D. Accounts Receivable			
E. Inventory			
F. Other			
Totals	$	$	$

PREVIOUS SBA OR OTHER GOVERNMENT FINANCING: If you or any principals or affiliates have ever requested Government Financing, complete the following:

Name of Agency	Original Amount of Loan	Date of Request	Approved or Declined	Balance	Current or Past Due
	$			$	
	$			$	

INDEBTEDNESS: Furnish the following information on all installment debts, contracts, notes, and mortgages payable. Indicate by an asterisk (*) items to be paid by loan proceeds and reason for paying same (present balance should agree with latest balance sheet submitted).

To Whom Payable	Original Amount	Original Date	Present Balance	Rate of Interest	Maturity Date	Monthly Payment	Security	Current or Past Due
	$		$			$		
	$		$			$		
	$		$			$		
	$		$			$		

MANAGEMENT (Proprietor, partners, officers, directors and all holders of outstanding stock — <u>100% of ownership must be shown</u>). Use separate sheet if necessary.

Name and Social Security Number	Complete Address	% Owned	*Military Service From	To	*Race	*Sex

* This data is collected for statistical purposes only. It has no bearing on the credit decision to approve or decline this application.

ASSISTANCE   List the name(s) and occupation(s) of any who assisted in preparation of this form, other than applicant.

Name and Occupation	Address	Total Fees Paid	Fees Due
Name and Occupation	Address	Total Fees Paid	Fees Due

Signature of Preparers if Other Than Applicant

THE FOLLOWING EXHIBITS MUST BE COMPLETED WHERE APPLICABLE. ALL QUESTIONS ANSWERED ARE MADE A PART OF THE APPLICATION.

For Guaranty Loans please provide an original and one copy (Photocopy is Acceptable) of the Application Form, and all Exhibits to the participating lender. For Direct Loans submit one original copy of application and Exhibits to SBA.

Submit SBA Form 1261 (Statements Required by Laws and Executive Orders). This form must be signed and dated by each Proprietor, Partner, Principal or Guarantor.

1. Submit SBA Form 912 (Personal History Statement) for each person e.g. owners, partners, officers, directors, major stockholders, etc.; the instructions are on SBA Form 912.

2. Furnish a signed current personal balance sheet (SBA Form 413 may be used for this purpose) for each stockholder (with 20% or greater ownership), partner, officer, and owner. Social Security number should be included on personal financial statement. Label this Exhibit B.

3. Include the statements listed below: 1, 2, 3 for the last three years; also 1, 2, 3, 4 dated within 90 days of filing the application; and statement 5, if applicable. This is Exhibit C (SBA has Management Aids that help in the preparation of financial statements.) All information must be signed and dated.

1. Balance Sheet   2. Profit and Loss Statement
3. Reconciliation of Net Worth
4. Aging of Accounts Receivable and Payable
5. Earnings projections for at least one year where financial statements for the last three years are unavailable or where requested by District Office.
   (If Profit and Loss Statement is not available, explain why and substitute Federal Income Tax Forms.)

4. Provide a brief history of your company and a paragraph describing the expected benefits it will receive from the loan. Label it Exhibit D.

Complete Small Business Loan Kit/121

5. Provide a brief description of the educational, technical and business background for all the people listed under Management. Please mark it Exhibit E.

6. Do you have any co-signers and/or guarantors for this loan? If so, please submit their names, addresses and personal balance sheet(s) as Exhibit F.

7. Are you buying machinery or equipment with your loan money? If so, you must include a list of the equipment and cost as quoted by the seller and his name and address. This is Exhibit G.

8. Have you or any officers of your company ever been involved in bankruptcy or insolvency proceedings? If so, please provide the details as Exhibit H. If none, check here: ☐ Yes ☐ No

9. Are you or your business involved in any pending lawsuits? If yes, provide the details as Exhibit I. If none, check here: ☐ Yes ☐ No

10. Do you or your spouse or any member of your household, or anyone who owns, manages, or directs your business or their spouses or members of their households work for the Small Business Administration, Small Business Advisory Council, SCORE or ACE, any Federal Agency, or the participating lender? If so, please provide the name and address of the person and the office where employed. label this Exhibit J. If none, check here: ☐ Yes ☐ No

11. Does your business, its owners or majority stockholders own or have a controlling interest in other businesses? If yes, please provide their names and the relationship with your company along with a current balance sheet and operating statement for each. This should be Exhibit K.

12. Do you buy from, sell to, or use the services of any concern in which someone in your company has a significant financial interest? If yes, provide details on a separate sheet of paper labeled Exhibit L.

13. If your business is a franchise, include a copy of the franchise agreement and a copy of the FTC disclosure statement supplied to you by the Franchisor. Please include it as Exhibit M.

CONSTRUCTION LOANS ONLY

14. Include a separate exhibit (Exhibit N) the estimated cost of the project and a statement of the source of any additional funds.

15. File the necessary compliance document (SBA Form 601).

16. Provide copies of preliminary construction plans and specifications. Include them as Exhibit O. Final plans will be required prior to disbursement.

DIRECT LOANS ONLY

17. Include two bank declination letters with your application. These letters should include the name and telephone number of the persons contacted at the banks, the amount and terms of the loan, the reason for decline and whether or not the bank will participate with SBA. In cities with 200,000 people or less, one letter will be sufficient.

EXPORT LOANS

18. Does your business presently engage in Export Trade? Check here ☐ Yes ☐ No

19. Do you plan to begin exporting as a result of this loan? Check here ☐ Yes ☐ No

20. Would you like information on Exporting? Check here ☐ Yes ☐ No

AGREEMENTS AND CERTIFICATIONS

Agreements of Nonemployment of SBA Personnel: I/We agree that if SBA approves this loan application I/We will not, for at least two years, hire as an employee or consultant anyone that was employed by the SBA during the one year period prior to the disbursement of the loan.

Certification: I/We certify: (a) I/We have not paid anyone connected with the Federal Government for help in getting this loan. I/We also agree to report to the SBA office of the Inspector General, 1441 L Street N.W., Washington, D.C. 20416 any Federal Government employee who offers, in return for any type of compensation, to help get this loan approved.

(b) All information in this application and the Exhibits are true and complete to the best of my/our knowledge and are submitted to SBA so SBA can decide whether to grant a loan or participate with a lending institution in a loan to me/us. I/We agree to pay for or reimburse SBA for the cost of any surveys, title or mortgage examinations, appraisals etc., performed by non-SBA personnel provided I/We have given my/our consent.

I/We understand that I/We need not pay anybody to deal with SBA. I/We have read and understand Form 394 which explains SBA policy on representatives and their fees.

If you make a statement that you know to be false or if you over value a security in order to help obtain a loan under the provisions of the Small Business Act, you can be fined up to $5,000 or be put in jail for up to two years, or both.

If Applicant is a proprietor or general partner, sign below:

By: _____
                                                    Date

If Applicant is a Corporation, sign below:

_____
Corporate Name and Seal   Date

_____

By: _____
                        Signature of President

Attested by: _____
                    Signature of Corporate Secretary

UNITED STATES SMALL BUSINESS ADMINISTRATION

SCHEDULE OF COLLATERAL

Exhibit A

Applicant		
Street Address		
City	State	Zip Code

LIST ALL COLLATERAL TO BE USED AS SECURITY FOR THIS LOAN

Section I—REAL ESTATE

Attach a copy of the deed(s) containing a full legal description of the land and show the location (street address) and city where the deed(s) is recorded. Following the address below, give a brief description of the improvements, such as size, type of construction, use, number of stories, and present condition (use additional sheet if more space is required).

LIST PARCELS OF REAL ESTATE					
Address	Year Acquired	Original Cost	Market Value	Amount of Lien	Name of Lienholder

Description(s):

Complete Small Business Loan Kit/123

SECTION II—PERSONAL PROPERTY

All items listed herein must show manufacturer or make, model, year, and serial number. Items with no serial number must be clearly identified (use additional sheet if more space is required).

Description - Show Manufacturer, Model. Serial No.	Year Acquired	Original Cost	Market Value	Current Lien Balance	Name of Lienholder

All information contained herein is TRUE and CORRECT to the best of my knowledge. I understand that FALSE statements may result in forfeiture of benefits and possible fine and prosecution by the U.S. Attorney General (Ref. 18 U.S.C. 100).

_____   Date _____

_____   Date _____

United States of America

SMALL BUSINESS ADMINISTRATION

STATEMENT OF PERSONAL HISTORY

Name and Address of Applicant (Firm Name)(Street, City, State and ZIP Code)	SBA District Office and City
	Amount Applied for

1 Personal Statement of (State name in full, if no middle name, state (NMN), or if initial only, indicate initial. List all former names used, and dates each name was used. Use separate sheet if necessary	2 Date of Birth: (Month, day and year)	
	3 Place of Birth (City & State or Foreign Country)	
First Middle Last	U.S. Citizen? ☐ YES ☐ NO If no, give alien registration number: #	
4. Give the percentage of ownership or stock owned or to be owned in the small business concern or the Development Company	Social Security No.	
5 Present residence address: From: To: Address:	City	State
Home Telephone No. (Include A/C):	Business Telephone No. (Include A/C):	
Immediate past residence address: From: To: Address:		

BE SURE TO ANSWER THE NEXT 3 QUESTIONS CORRECTLY BECAUSE THEY ARE IMPORTANT.

THE FACT THAT YOU HAVE AN ARREST OR CONVICTION RECORD WILL NOT NECESSARILY DISQUALIFY YOU. BUT AN INCORRECT ANSWER WILL PROBABLY CAUSE YOUR APPLICATION TO BE TURNED DOWN.

6. Are you presently under indictment, on parole or probation?

☐ Yes ☐ No   If yes, furnish details in a separate exhibit. List name(s) under which held, if applicable

7. Have you ever been charged with or arrested for any criminal offense other than a minor motor vehicle violation?

☐ Yes ☐ No   If yes, furnish details in a separate exhibit. List name(s) under which charged, if applicable

8. Have you ever been convicted of any criminal offense other than a minor motor vehicle violation?

☐ Yes ☐ No   If yes, furnish details in a separate exhibit. List name(s) under which convicted, if applicable

9 Name and address of participating bank

The information on this form will be used in connection with an investigation of your character. Any information you wish to submit, that you feel will expedite this investigation should be set forth.

Whoever makes any statement knowing it to be false, for the purpose of obtaining for himself or for any applicant, any loan, or loan extension by renewal, deferment or otherwise, or for the purpose of obtaining, or influencing SBA toward, anything of value under the Small Business Act, as amended, shall be punished under Section 16(a) of that Act, by a fine of not more than $5000, or by imprisonment for not more than 2 years, or both.

Signature	Title	Date

Complete Small Business Loan Kit/125

PERSONAL FINANCIAL STATEMENT

As of _____ 19 ____

Complete this form if 1) a sole proprietorship by the proprietor; 2) a partnership by each partner; 3) a corporation by each officer and each stockholder with 20% or more ownership; 4) any other person or entity providing a guaranty on the loan.

Name _____ Residence Phone _____

Residence Address _____

City, State, & Zip _____

Business Name of Applicant/Borrower _____

ASSETS (Omit Cents)		LIABILITIES (Omit Cents)	
Cash on hand & in Banks.................. $_____		Accounts Payable .... $_____	
Savings Accounts....................... _____		Notes Payable (to Bk & Others	
IRA.................................. _____		(Describe in Section 2)................... _____	
Accounts & Notes Receivable		Installment Account (Auto)	
(Describe in Section 6) .... _____		Mo. Payments $_____ _____	
Life Insurance—Cash		Installment Account (Other)	
Surrender Value Only .... _____		Mo. Payments $ _____ _____	
Stocks and Bonds		Loans on Life Insurance .... _____	
(Describe in Section 3) .... _____		Mortgages on Real Estate..................	
Real Estate		(Describe in Section 4)...................	
(Describe in Section 4) .... _____		Unpaid Taxes	
Automobile—Present Value .... _____		(Describe in Section 7)................... _____	
Other Personal Property		Other Liabilities	
(Describe in Section 5) .... _____		(Describe in Section 8)................... _____	
Other Assets			
(Describe in Section 6) .... _____		Total Liabilities........................... _____	
		Net Worth .... _____	
Total.......................... $_____		Total .... $_____	

Section 1. Source of Income

Contingent Liabilities

Salary .... $_____	As Endorser or Co-Maker .... $_____	
Net Investment Income .... _____	Legal Claims & Judgments .... _____	
Real Estate Income .... _____	Provision for Fed Income Tax........................... _____	
Other Income (Describe)*........... _____	Other Special Debt .... _____	

Description of Items Listed in Section I _____

*(Alimony or child support payments need not be disclosed in "Other Income" unless it is desired to have such payments counted toward total income.)

Section 2. Notes Payable to Banks and Others

Name & Address of Noteholder	Original Balance	Current Balance	Payment Amount	Terms (Monthly-etc.)	How Secured or Endorsed—Type of Collateral

Section 3. Stocks and Bonds: (*Use separate sheet if necessary*)

No. of Shares	Names of Securities	Cost	Market Value Quotation/Exchange	Date Amount

Section 4. Real Estate Owned. (*List each parcel separately. Use supplemental sheets if necessary. Each sheet must be identified as a supplement to this statement and signed*).

Address—Type of property	Title is in name of	Date Purchased	Original Cost	Present Value	Mortgage Balance	Amount of Payment	Status of Mortgage

Section 5. Other Personal Property. (*Describe, and if any is mortgaged, state name and address of mortgage holder and amount of mortgage, terms of payment, and if delinquent, describe delinquency.*)

Section 6. Other Assets, Notes & Accounts Receivable (*Describe*)

Section 7. Unpaid Taxes. (*Describe in detail, as to type, to whom payable, when due, amount, and what, if any, property the tax lien attaches*)

Section 8. Other Liabilities. (*Describe in detail*)

Section 9. Life Insurance Held (*Give face amount of policies—name of company and beneficiaries*)

SBA/Lender is authorized to make all inquiries deemed necessary to verify the accuracy of the statements made herein and to determine my/our creditworthiness.

(I) or (We) certify the above and the statements contained in the schedules herein are a true and accurate statement of (my) or (our) financial condition as of the date stated herein. This statement is given for the purpose of: (*Check one of the following*)

☐ Inducing S.B.A. to grant a loan as requested in the application, to the individual or firm whose name appears herein.
☐ Furnishing a statement of (my) or (our) financial condition, pursuant to the terms of the guaranty executed by (me) or (us) at the same time S.B.A. granted a loan to the individual or firm, whose name appears herein.

Signature	Signature	Date

SOCIAL SECURITY NO.	SOCIAL SECURITY NO.

SBA

LOANS FOR VIETNAM-ERA AND DISABLED VETERANS

The Program SBA offers a broad range of loan programs to all veterans. Most of these loans are made by financial institutions and guaranteed by SBA. Regular business loans usually do not exceed $350,000 and are made only if financing is not available from other sources on reasonable terms. Special consideration is offered all veterans who apply for regular business loans.

Under a special loan program, funds are available for direct loans to disabled and Vietnam-era veterans. The same criteria are used as in the regular business loan program. These loans may be made to establish a small firm or assist in the operation or expansion of an existing business. The administrative ceiling on these loans is $150,000. SBA cannot make a direct loan if a guaranteed loan or other credit is available.

Eligibility All veterans must meet SBA standard loan criteria. They must first seek private financing before applying to SBA; show ability to run a business successfully; own and operate at least 51 percent of the firm; and have enough capital involved to operate on a sound financial basis. Veterans who meet SBA loan criteria are placed ahead of non-veterans who apply the same day, if their applications are complete.

Vietnam-era veterans are those veterans who served for a period of more than 180 days, any part of which was between August 5, 1964 and May 7m, 1975, and were discharged other than dishonorably; and Vietnam-era veterans discharged for service-connected disability; disabled veterans are those veterans with compensable 30 percent or more disability; or, veterans with a disability discharge.

Collateral Loans must be of such sound value or so secured as reasonably to assure repayment. Available collateral and other guarantees will be required.

How to Apply All applications should be submitted to the nearest SBA office. More detailed information may be obtained from the Veterans Affairs Officer at any SBA office.

Issued by: Public Communications
Revised: November 1983

U.S. SMALL BUSINESS ADMINISTRATION

REQUEST FOR COUNSELING

Please Print

Name of Company	Name of Inquirer	Telephone #

Street	City	State	County	Zip

Employer ID #	Social Security Number	Veteran	Vietnam Era Veteran
▯▯▮▯▯▯▯▯▯	▯▯▯ ▯▯ ▯▯▯▯	Yes ☐ No ☐	Yes ☐ No ☐ Discharged

Are you presently:	Yes	No	Can you furnish a recent:		Yes	No
In Business?	☐	☐	Balance Sheet?		☐	☐
Starting a Business?	☐	☐	Profit & Loss Statement?		☐	☐
SBA Borrower?	☐	☐				

Kind of business/services (Please specify)

Retail (Selling) _____   Construction _____

Service (Kind) _____   Wholesale (Selling) _____

Manufacturing (Product) _____   Other (Specify) _____

Check the problem areas for which you seek assistance.

☐ 1. Starting a New Business
☐ 2. Sources of Credit and Financing
☐ 3. Increasing Sales
☐ 4. Advertising & Sales Promotion
☐ 5. Market Research
☐ 6. Selling to the Government
☐ 7. Bidding and Estimating
☐ 8. International Trade

☐ 9. Recordkeeping and Accounting
☐ 10. Financial Statements
☐ 11. Office or Plant Management
☐ 12. Personnel
☐ 13. Engineering and Research
☐ 14. Inventory Control
☐ 15. Purchasing
☐ 16. Credit & Collections

Please describe how SBA may be of assistance.

I request management assistance from the Small Business Administration. I understand that this assistance is free of charge. I agree to cooperate should I be selected to participate in surveys designed to evaluate SBA assistance services. I authorize SBA to furnish relevant information to the assigned management counselor although I expect that information to be held in strict confidence by him/her.

I further understand that any counselor has agreed not to: (1) recommend goods or services from sources in which he/she has an interest and (2) accept fees or commissions developing from this counseling relationship. In consideration of SBA's furnishing management or technical assistance, I waive all claims against SBA personnel or counselors arising from this assistance.

Signature and Title of Requestor	Date

WORKSHEET NO. 2

ESTIMATED MONTHLY EXPENSES

Item	Your estimate of monthly expenses based on sales of $_____ per year	Your estimate of how much cash you need to start your business (See column 3.)	What to put in column 2 (These figures are typical for one kind of business. you will have to decide how many months to allow for in your business.)
	Column 1	Column 2	Column 3
Salary of owner-manager	$	$	2 times column 1
All other salaries and wages			3 times column 1
Rent			3 times column 1
Advertising			3 times column 1
Delivery expense			3 times column 1
Supplies			3 times column 1
Telephone and telegraph			3 times column 1
Other utilities			3 times column 1
Insurance			Payment required by insurance company
Taxes, including Social Security			4 times column 1
Interest			3 times column 1
Maintenance			3 times column 1

Item		Instructions
Legal and other professional fees		3 times column 1
Miscellaneous		3 times column 1
STARTING COSTS YOU ONLY HAVE TO PAY ONCE		Leave column 2 blank
Fixtures and equipment		Fill in worksheet 3 on page 12 and put the total here
Decorating and remodeling		Talk it over with a contractor
Installation of fixtures and equipment		Talk to suppliers from who you buy these
Starting inventory		Suppliers will probably help you estimate this
Deposits with public utilities		Find out from utilities companies
Legal and other professional fees		Lawyer, accountant, and so on
Licenses and permits		Find out from city offices what you have to have
Advertising and promotion for opening		Estimate what you'll use
Accounts receivable		What you need to buy more stock until credit customers pay
Cash		For unexpected expenses or losses, special purchases, etc.
Other		Make a separate list and enter total
TOTAL ESTIMATED CASH YOU NEED TO START WITH	$	Add up all the numbers in column 2

SBA   Directory of Business Development Publications

THANK YOU

for your interest in the Small Business Administration. We are pleased to offer you our extensive library of business publications.

INFORMATION is power! It is an asset that can help overcome uncertainty and open new avenues for opportunity. SUCCESS in your business will depend on what you know and how well you apply what you have learned.

- *In 1986, the SBA distributed over 6.2 million business publications to entrepreneurs like yourself.*

- *All SBA business publications are Easy-To-Read and provide Basic Information about starting, running or expanding a successful small business.*

- *The practical guidance found in these publications can provide you with knowledge about successful small business management.*

Review the following publications and select those that can best satisfy your business needs.

FINANCIAL MANAGEMENT AND ANALYSIS

FM 1 ABC's OF BORROWING *
Some small business people cannot understand why a lending institution refused to lend them money. Others have no trouble getting funds but are surprised to find strings attached to their loans. Learn the fundamentals of borrowing....$1.00.

FM 2 PROFIT COSTING AND PRICING FOR MANUFACTURERS
Uncover the latest techniques for pricing your products profitably....$1.00.

FM 3 BASIC BUDGETS FOR PROFIT PLANNING *
This publication takes the worry out of putting together a comprehensive budgeting system to monitor your profits and assess your financial operations.....50¢.

FM 4 UNDERSTANDING CASH FLOW
In order to survive, a business must have enough cash to meet its obligations. This Aid shows the owner/manager how to plan for the movement of cash through the business and thus plan for future requirements....$1.00.

FM 5 A VENTURE CAPITAL PRIMER FOR SMALL BUSINESS
This best-seller highlights the venture capital resources available and how to develop a proposal for obtaining these funds.....50¢.

FM 6 ACCOUNTING SERVICES FOR SMALL SERVICE FIRMS
Sample profit/loss statements are used to illustrate how accounting services can help expose and correct trouble spots in a business' financial records....50¢.

FM 7 ANALYZE YOUR RECORDS TO REDUCE COSTS
Cost reduction IS NOT simply slashing any and all expenses. Understand the nature of expenses and how they inter-relate with sales, inventories, and profits. Achieve greater profits through more efficient use of the dollar.....50¢.

* — DENOTES OUR BEST-SELLERS !

FM 8 BUDGETING IN A SMALL BUSINESS FIRM
Learn how to set up and keep sound financial records. Study how to effectively use journals, ledgers and charts to increase profits.....50¢.

FM 9 SOUND CASH MANAGEMENT AND BORROWING
Avoid a "cash crisis" through proper use of cash budgets, cash flow projections and planned borrowing concepts.....50¢.

FM 10 RECORDKEEPING IN A SMALL BUSINESS *
Need some basic advice on setting up a useful recordkeeping system? This publication describes how....$1.00.

FM 11 BREAKEVEN ANALYSIS: A DECISION MAKING TOOL
Learn how "breakeven analysis" enables the manager/owner to make better decisions concerning sales, profits and costs....$1.00.

FM 12 A PRICING CHECKLIST FOR SMALL RETAILERS
The owner/manager of a small retail business can use this checklist to uncover proven pricing strategies that can lead to profits.....50¢.

FM 13 PRICING YOUR PRODUCTS AND SERVICES PROFITABLY
Discusses how to price your products profitably, how to use the various techniques of pricing and when to use these techniques to your advantage....$1.00.

GENERAL MANAGEMENT AND PLANNING

MP 1 EFFECTIVE BUSINESS COMMUNICATIONS
Explains the importance of business communications and how they play a valuable role in business success.....50¢.

* — DENOTES OUR BEST-SELLERS !

MP 2 LOCATING OR RELOCATING YOUR BUSINESS
Learn how a company's market, available labor force, transportation and raw materials are affected when selecting a business location....$1.00.

MP 3 PROBLEMS IN MANAGING A FAMILY—OWNED BUSINESS
Specific problems exist when attempting to make a family-owned businesses successful. This publication offers suggestions on how to overcoem these difficulties....50.

MP 4 BUSINESS PLAN FOR SMALL MANUFACTURERS
Designed to help an owner/manager of a small manufacturing firm. This publication covers all the basic information necessary to develop an effective business plan....$1.00.

MP 5 BUSINESS PLAN FOR SMALL CONSTRUCTION FIRMS
This publication is designed to help an owner/manager of a small construction company pull together the resources to develop a business plan....$1.00.

MP 6 PLANNING AND GOAL SETTING FOR SMALL BUSINESS *
Learn how to plan for success....50¢.

MP 7 FIXING PRODUCTION MISTAKES
Structured as a checklist, this publication emphasizes the steps that should be taken by a manufacturer when a production mistake has been found....50¢.

MP 8 SHOULD YOU LEASE OR BUY EQUIPMENT?
Describes various aspects of the lease/buy decision. It lists advantages and disadvantages of leasing and provides a format for comparing the costs of the two....50¢.

MP 9 BUSINESS PLAN FOR RETAILERS
Learn how to develop a business plan for a retail business....$1.00.

* — DENOTES OUR BEST-SELLERS !

MP 10 CHOOSING A RETAIL LOCATION
Learn about current retail site selection techniques such as demographic and traffic analysis. This publication addresses the hard questions the retailer must answer before making the choice of a store location....$1.00.

MP 11 BUSINESS PLAN FOR SMALL SERVICE FIRMS
Outlines the key points to be included in the business plan of a small service firm....50¢.

MP 12 GOING INTO BUSINESS *
This best-seller highlights important considerations you should know in reaching a decision to start your own business. It also includes a checklist for going into business....50¢.

MP 13 FEASIBILITY CHECKLIST FOR STARTING YOUR OWN BUSINESS
Helps you determine if your idea represents a real business opportunity. Assists you in screening out ideas that are likely to fail before you invest extensive time, money and effort in them....$1.00.

MP 14 HOW TO GET STARTED WITH A SMALL BUSINESS COMPUTER
Helps you forecast your computer needs, evaluate the alternative choices and select the right computer system for your business....$1.00.

MP 15 THE BUSINESS PLAN FOR HOMEBASED BUSINESS *
Provides a comprehensive approach to developing a business plan for a homebased business. If you are convinced that a profitable home business is attainable, this publication will provide a step-by-step guide to develop a plan for your business....$1.00.

MP 16 HOW TO BUY OR SELL A BUSINESS
Learn several techniques used in determining the best price to buy or sell a small business....$1.00.

MP 17 PURCHASING FOR OWNERS OF SMALL PLANTS
Presents an outline of an effective purchasing program. Also includes a bibliography for further research into industrial purchasing....50¢.

* — DENOTES OUR BEST-SELLERS !

MT 4 MARKETING CHECKLIST FOR SMALL RETAILERS

This checklist is for the owner/manager of a small retail business. The questions outlined cover customer analysis, buying, pricing and promotion and other factors in the retail marketing process....$1.00.

MT 5 ADVERTISING GUIDELINES FOR SMALL RETAIL FIRMS

These guidelines include how to plan the advertising budget, select the appropriate media, use cooperative advertising and prepare advertisements....50¢.

MT 6 ADVERTISING MEDIA DECISIONS *

Discover how to effectively target your product or service to the proper market. This publication also discusses the different advertising media and how to select and use the best media vehicle for your business....$1.00.

MT 7 PLAN YOUR ADVERTISING BUDGET

Describes some simple methods for establishing an advertising budget and suggests ways of changing budget amounts to get the effect you want....50¢.

MT 8 RESEARCH YOUR MARKET *

Learn what market research is and how you can benefit from it. Introduces inexpensive techniques that small business owners can apply to gather facts about their existing customer base and how to expand it....$1.00.

MT 9 SELLING BY MAIL ORDER

Provides basic information on how to run a successful mail order business. Includes information on product selection, pricing, testing and writing effective advertisements....$1.00.

MT 10 MARKET OVERSEAS WITH U.S. GOVERNMENT HELP

Entering the overseas marketplace offers exciting opportunities to increase company sales and profits. Learn about the programs available to help small businesses break into the world of exporting....$1.00.

* — DENOTES OUR BEST-SELLERS !

PERSONNEL MANAGEMENT

PM 1 CHECKLIST FOR DEVELOPING A TRAINING PROGRAM

Describes a step-by-step process of setting up an effective employee training program....50¢.

PM 2 EMPLOYEES: HOW TO FIND AND PAY THEM

A business is only as good as the people in it. Learn how to find and hire the right employees....$1.00.

PM 3 STAFFING YOUR STORE

Discusses the process of staffing a small retail business, setting personnel policies, determining what skill level and abilities are needed, finding applicants and interviewing techniques....50¢.

PM 4 MANAGING EMPLOYEE BENEFITS

Describes employee benefits as one part of the total compensation package and discusses proper management of benefits....$1.00.

NEW PRODUCTS/IDEAS/INVENTIONS

PI 1 CAN YOU MAKE MONEY WITH YOUR IDEA OR INVENTION?

This publication is a step-by-step guide which shows how you can make money by turning your creative ideas into marketable products. It is a resource for entrepreneurs attempting to establish themselves in the marketplace....50¢.

PI 2 INTRODUCTION TO PATENTS

Offers some basic facts about patents to help clarify your rights. It discusses the relationships among a business, an inventor and the Patent and Trademark Office to ensure protection of your product and to avoid or win infringement suits....50¢.

MP 18 BUYING FOR RETAIL STORES
Discusses the latest trends in retail buying. Includes a bibliography that references a wide variety of private and public sources of information on most aspects of retail buying....$1.00.

MP 19 SMALL BUSINESS DECISION MAKING
Acquaint yourself with the wealth of information available on management approaches and techniques to identify, analyze and solve business problems....$1.00

MP 20 BUSINESS CONTINUATION PLANNING
Provides an overview of business owners' life insurance needs that are not typically considered until after the death of one of the business' principal owners....$1.00.

MP 21 DEVELOPING A STRATEGIC BUSINESS PLAN *
Helps you develop a formal strategic plan of action for your small business....$1.00

MP 22 INVENTORY MANAGEMENT
Discusses the purpose of inventory management, types of inventories, recordkeeping and forecasting inventory levels....50¢.

MP 23 TECHNIQUES FOR PROBLEM SOLVING
Instructs the small business person on the key techniques of problem solving and problem identification, as well as designing and implementing a plan to correct these problems....$1.00

MP 24 TECHNIQUES FOR PRODUCTIVITY IMPROVEMENT
Learn how to increase worker output through motivating "quality of work life" concepts and tailoring benefits to meet the needs of the employees....$1.00.

MP 25 SELECTING THE LEGAL STRUCTURE FOR YOUR BUSINESS
Discusses the various legal structures that a small business can use in setting up its operations. It briefly identifies the types of legal structures and lists the advantages and disadvantages of each....50¢.

* — DENOTES OUR BEST-SELLERS !

MP 26 EVALUATING FRANCHISE OPPORTUNITIES
Although the success rate for franchise-owned businesses is significantly better than start-up businesses, success is not guaranteed. Learn how to evaluate franchise opportunities and select the business that's right for you....50¢.

CRIME PREVENTION

CP 1 REDUCING SHOPLIFTING LOSSES
Learn the latest techniques on how to spot, deter, apprehend and prosecute shoplifters....50¢.

CP 2 CURTAILING CRIME—INSIDE AND OUT
Positive steps can be taken to curb crime. They include safeguards against employee dishonesty and ways to control shoplifting. In addition, this publication includes measures to outwit bad-check passing and ways to prevent burglary and robbery....$1.00.

MARKETING

MT 1 CREATIVE SELLING: THE COMPETITIVE EDGE *
Explains how to use creative selling techniques to increase profits....50¢.

MT 2 MARKETING FOR SMALL BUSINESS: AN OVERVIEW *
Provides an overview of the "Marketing" concept and contains an extensive bibliography of sources covering the subject of marketing....$1.00.

MT 3 IS THE INDEPENDENT SALES AGENT FOR YOU?
Provides guidelines that help the owner manager of a small company determine whether or not a sales agent is needed and pointers on how to choose one....50¢.

* — DENOTES OUR BEST-SELLERS !

ORDER FORM FOR PUBLICATIONS

ITEM#	QTY	PRICE	TOTAL
FM 1	____	$1.00	_____
FM 2	____	1.00	_____
FM 3	____	.50	_____
FM 4	____	1.00	_____
FM 5	____	.50	_____
FM 6	____	.50	_____
FM 7	____	.50	_____
FM 8	____	.50	_____
FM 9	____	.50	_____
FM 10	____	1.00	_____
FM 11	____	1.00	_____
FM 12	____	.50	_____
FM 13	____	1.00	_____
MP 1	____	.50	_____
MP 2	____	1.00	_____
MP 3	____	.50	_____
MP 4	____	1.00	_____
MP 5	____	1.00	_____
MP 6	____	.50	_____
MP 7	____	.50	_____
MP 8	____	.50	_____
MP 9	____	1.00	_____
MP 10	____	1.00	_____
MP 11	____	.50	_____
MP 12	____	.50	_____
MP 13	____	1.00	_____
MP 14	____	1.00	_____
MP 15	____	1.00	_____
MP 16	____	1.00	_____
MP 17	____	.50	_____
MP 18	____	1.00	_____
MP 19	____	1.00	_____
MP 20	____	1.00	_____
MP 21	____	1.00	_____
MP 22	____	.50	_____
MP 23	____	1.00	_____
MP 24	____	1.00	_____
MP 25	____	.50	_____
MP 26	____	.50	_____

Continued on next page.

ITEM#	QTY	PRICE	TOTAL
CP 1	____	.50	____
CP 2	____	1.00	____
MT 1	____	.50	____
MT 2	____	1.00	____
MT 3	____	.50	____
MT 4	____	1.00	____
MT 5	____	.50	____
MT 6	____	1.00	____
MT 7	____	.50	____
MT 8	____	1.00	____
MT 9	____	1.00	____
MT 10	____	1.00	____
PM 1	____	.50	____
PM 2	____	1.00	____
PM 3	____	.50	____
PM 4	____	1.00	____
PI 1	____	.50	____
PI 2	____	.50	____

Total Amount Due SBA _____

NAME _____

STREET _____

CITY, STATE, ZIP CODE _____

HOW TO ORDER

1. Check the titles you want.

2. Tear along the perforated line and complete the order form.

3. Make your check or money order payable to:
   U.S. Small Business Administration
   (NOTE: No cash, credit cards or purchase orders).

4. Mail the order form with your payment to:
   U.S. Small Business Administration
   P.O. Box 15434
   Fort Worth, Texas 76119

THANK YOU

GLOSSARY
OF COMMON
BUSINESS
TERMS

Note: the definitions offered here are intended to provide a general working understanding of the terms, rather than precise technical meanings.

Accelerated Depreciation

Any depreciation method that provides for larger depreciation deductions in the early years of a project's life.

Accounts Payable

Money owed to suppliers.

Accounts Receivable

Money owed by customers.

Accounts Receivable Financing

Short-term financing to obtain cash based on outstanding accounts receivable.

Active Corps of Executives (ACE)

Program sponsored by the Small Business Administration; business executives volunteer their consulting assistance to small businesses.

Amortization

Repayment of loan by installments.

Assets

The resources, properties or property rights owned by an individual or firm. An asset embodies probably future benefit and the ability to contribute directly or indirectly to future income.

Balance Sheet

An itemized statement of a firm's financial position at a given point in time. Total assets equal total liabilities plus owners' equity.

Bidders Mailing List

Lists compiled by federal government agencies of businesses that wish to receive information on invitations for bids.

Blue Sky Laws

State laws covering the issue and trading of securities.

Bond

Long-term debt.

Bootstrap Financing

Obtaining finances from internal sources such as customers, mortgages, suppliers, and tighter management control.

Break-Even Analysis

Analysis undertaken to determine the level of sales at which a project's income would just equal costs. Break-even analysis shows the relationship between profits, fixed costs, variable costs, and volume.

Break-Even Point

The number of units that must be sold at a specified price to cover the fixed and variable costs. Any units sold above the break-even point contribute to profit.

Business Overhead Expenses

The operating expenses of a business, including costs of rent, utilities, interior decoration, and taxes--and excluding labor and materials.

Capital Budget

List of planned investment expenditures and the timing of such expenditures.

Capital Repatriation

When a company operating in a foreign country transfers money or property back to its home country. Some foreign governments restrict this action to prevent a drain of capital or exploitation by foreign firms.

Cash Flow Statement

A summary of all cash transactions during a certain period. It is useful as a budgeting tool and for management's internal financial planning and control.

Certificate of Deposit

A statement from a bank certifying that the named person has a specified sum on deposit.

Certified Public Accountant (C.P.A.)

An accountant who has passed the requirements to be licensed as a public accountant. Each state has its own education, experience, and moral requirements for certification.

Chartered Life Underwriter (C.L.U.)

An agent who has taken additional coursework to qualify for this advanced professional standing in selling property and casualty insurance.

Collateral

Assets that are given as security for a loan.

Common Shares

Those who own common shares in the corporation have residual claims on the corporation's assets and earnings after all debts and preferred shareholders' claims have been paid.

Controller

Company executive responsible for firms' budgetary, accounting, and auditing operations.

Convertible Security

Bond or preferred stock that may be converted to common stock.

Copyright

Legal protection for authors, composes, and artists from unauthorized duplication or reproduction of their original work.

Corporation

An organizational structure as an autonomous legal entity with transferable ownership.

Cost of Goods Sold

Costs that are incurred to produce or acquire the unites that are sold. It is derived from beginning inventory plus purchases minus ending inventory.

Current Asset

Asset that will normally be converted into cash within one year or within the normal operating cycle of the firm.

Current Liability

Liability that will normally be paid within one year or within the normal operating cycle of the firm.

Debt Warrant

The right for a debt holder to purchase common stock at a specified price in exchange for the outstanding debt.

Depreciation

Reduction in the book value of an asset. Can be deducted from taxable income.

Deviation Analysis

A comparison between actual and planned or budgeted figures. Highlights the deviations from expected operations and the areas where remedial action is necessary.

Direct Method Market Entry

The exporter retains responsibility for shipping her product, but may or may not retain responsibility for sales, regulations, marketing, and final distribution.

Dome Ledgers

Standardized forms for bookkeeping; provide a ready-made system for recording transactions.

Double Taxation

Corporate income is taxed and then taxed again as personal income when distributed to owners as dividends.

Draft on Foreign Buyer

The exporter may receive payment by presenting a check written against the buyer's account. The bank will either agree to pay its value when it matures or forward it to the buyer's foreign bank to hold until payment by the buyer.

EBIT

Earnings before income and taxes.

Executive Summary

A brief synopsis of a document that highlights the key facts, issues, and conclusions. It precedes the body of the document.

EPS

Earnings per share.

Equity

A company's net worth; the monetary value of the company that exceeds the claims against it.

Equity Financing

Raising funds by selling capital stock, rather than by incurring debt.

Factoring

That which occurs when a financial institution buys a firm's accounts receivable and collects the debt.

Financial Ratios

Ratios that measure either the liquidity, profitability, or performance of the business. Often used as a yardstick to compare companies in the same field.

Fiscal Year

A period of twelve consecutive months chosen by a business as its accounting period.

Fixed Costs

Expenses that do not vary with the volume of production or activity in the short run; costs that are incurred regardless of the level of sales.

Focus Group

A small representative group of people brought together to answer questions for a market survey.

Free Trade Zones

A designated secured area legally outside of a nation's customs territory where a trader may store, sell, manufacture, or repack goods without paying customs duties or internal revenue taxes unless the product is moved to a customs territory.

General Partner

A partner who agrees to share ownership of a business with full personal liability for the debts of the firm.

Generally Accepted Accounting Principles (GAAP)

The conventions, rules, and procedures defined by the Financial Accounting Standards Board as proper accounting methods.

Gross Margin

Sales minus cost of goods sold.

Income Statement

The statement of revenues, expenses, gains, losses, and taxes to calculate net income for the period.

Indirect Exporting

The exporter hires an intermediary to handle all phases of exporting, including shipping.

Insurance Agency

A group of agents that represent one or more specified insurance companies. The agency sells insurance policies offered only by those companies.

Inventory Financing

Loans based on unsold inventory. The loan is repaid when the goods are sold.

Investment Tax Credit

A federal government provision for reduction of tax liability when businesses purchase new equipment.

Invitation for Bids (IFB)

An announcement of contract work that is open for bids. The IFB outlines the specific requirements of the purchase.

Joint Venture

Investment in a project, plant, or facility with another firm. Often joint ventures in international business are necessitated by national laws prohibiting majority ownership by a foreign corporation.

Journal

The book of original entry where financial transactions are initially recorded.

Lease

Long-term (i.e., more than one year) rental agreement.

Ledger

Book of final entry containing all of the financial statement accounts.

Letter of Credit

Guarantee of payment upon proof of completion of the terms and conditions of the agreement. A common method of payment between banks for exports.

Liability

Present obligation to transfer assets (e.g., money) or provide services in the future as a result of past transactions or events (for example, payment owed suppliers).

Licensing

A contractual agreement between a business and another business or government (often foreign) to provide a product, technology, or knowledge for a specified fee.

Limited Partner

Partner with an ownership interest whose liabilities are limited to the share of ownership.

Line of Credit

Bank agreement allowing a company to borrow at any time up to a specified limit.

Liquid Assets

Assets most easily turned into cash.

Location Analysis

A study of the business environment to determine the optimal place to establish a business.

Lock-Box System

Customers send payments to a post office box; local bank collects and processes the checks; surplus funds are transferred to the firm's principal bank.

Market Position

The strategy pursued that establishes a business or product as either a leader, challenger, follower, or nicher in the marketplace.

Market Strategy

Based on the "Four P's"--product, price, promotion, and place (distribution). The policies in each of these four areas determine the specific marketing mix.

Marketable Securities

Stocks and bonds of other companies that the firm plans to sell for cash if needed.

Merger

The process wherein two companies combine assets; liabilities of the selling company are absorbed by the buyer.

Net Income

Revenues minus cost of goods sold, expenses, and taxes for a specified period.

Net Present Value

A project's net contribution to the firm's wealth. The present value of all future income from the project minus the amount of investment.

Net Worth

Book value of shareholders' equity plus retained earnings.

One-Write System

A standardized bookkeeping system that allows the recording of each transaction with only one entry.

Opportunity Cost

The present value of the income that could be earned from using an asset in its best alternative use to the one being considered.

Patent

Legal document authorizing exclusive property rights to an invention of a product or process.

Portfolio Investment

Investment of capital with no interest in management or operational participation in the business.

Preferred Shares

Those shares that claim a priority on dividends before common shareholders receive a dividend. The dividend is usually a predetermined amount.

Present Value

Value of future cash flows in today's values.

Price Elasticity

The extent to which a change in price will cause a change in demand.   For example, if prices are inelastic, consumers will continue to buy the same amount of an item regardless of increases or decreases in prices.   On the other hadn, an sharp rise in elastic prices will cause a drop in demand.

Prime Rate

Interest Rate at which banks lend to their most favored customers.

Procurement Automated Source System (PASS)

A computerized listing of small businesses compiled by the Small Business Administration that is used as a resource base for federal procurement centers and prime contractors.

Product Brand Management

The development and implementation of a marketing strategy for a particular product brand.

Product Factors

Key factors that influence demand for a given product.

Public Stock Offering

A method to raise equity funds by selling shares in the corporation to the public.   A public company's shares are traded on the stock exchange.

Remittance of Profits

The act of transferring profits earned in a foreign country back to one's home country.

Requests for Proposals (RFPs)

Announcements of contract work open for proposals. The proposals then undergo a process of negotiation and modification before a contract is awarded.

Retained Earnings

Earnings not paid out as dividends.

Seed Financing

Initial funds to enable a business to establish itself and begin operations.

Service Corps of Retired Executives (SCORE)

Program sponsored by the Small Business Administration. Retired executives volunteer their time and expertise to assist small businesses.

Small Business Development Centers

A 26-state network of university- and college-based centers, which offer consulting services at no charge for small businesses and start-ups.

Sole Proprietorship

A business operated and owned by one individual.

Statement of Changes in Financial Position

This statement illustrates the sources and uses of funds during a specified period. The sources show how the firm obtained financing for its uses of funds, or investment requirements.

Subchapter S Corporation

A corporation with fewer than 25 shareholders, only one class of stock, at least 20% of its income generated domestically, and without any non-resident aliens as shareholders

Target Market

That segment of the market identified as a primary customer.

Trademark

Legal protection of a name or symbol of a product used in commerce.

Treasury Shares

Capital stock issued and then repurchased by the corporation.

Unsecured Loan

Loans that are not backed by any security or collateral.

Variable Costs

Costs that change with the volume of activity or sales. These costs are theoretically zero if there are no sales.

Variance Analysis

An analysis to explain the causes of deviation revealed in deviation analyses. The variance can be determined as due to either price or volume changes.

Venture Capital Firms

Firms that provide equity financing for new or untested businesses that are seen as likely to become highly profitable.

Working Capital

Current assets minus current liabilities.

SBA
PREFERRED
LENDERS

PREFERRED SBA LENDER STATUS

The SBA designates as preferred lenders certain banks that are interested in working with the SBA loan participation program. Special training programs teach employees of these banks the lending procedures and criteria of the SBA. Some banks are content to maintain the status of SBA lenders; however, preferred lenders will make the extra effort of hiring and training specialists who are fully versed in SBA procedures and evaluation criteria. These lenders can evaluate your loan package thoroughly and speak for the SBA regarding acceptance or rejection of a participation loan.

THE PREFERRED LENDER PROGRAM

Region I
(Connecticut, Massachusetts, Maine, and Vermont)

Region II
(New York, New Jersey)

Region III
(Pennsylvania, Virginia, West Virginia)

Region IV
(Alabama, Florida, Georgia, North Carolina, South Carolina, Mississippi)

Region V
(Illinois, Indiana, Michigan, Minnesota, Ohio, Wisconsin)

Region VI
(Arkansas, New Mexico, Louisiana, Oklahoma, Texas)

Region VII
(Iowa, Kansas, Missouri, Nebraska)

Region VIII
(Colorado, Montana, South Dakota, Utah, Wyoming)

Region IX
(Arizona, California, Hawaii, Nevada)

Region X
(Alaska, Idaho, Washington)

REGION I

Connecticut

Hamden: American National Bank

Waterbury: Colonial Bank

Massachusetts

Boston: First National Bank of Boston

Boston: Shawmut Bank

Peabody: Essexbank

Springfield: Bank of New England West

Worcester: Guaranty Bank & Trust Company

Maine

Augusta: Key Bank of Central Maine

Vermont

Brattleboro: Vermont National Bank

Burlington: Chittenden Bank

Burlington: The Merchants Bank

Randolph: Randolph National Bank

REGION II

New York

Albany: New York Business Development Corp.

Buffalo: Liberty National Bank & Trust Co.

Buffalo: Manufacturers & Traders Trust Co.

New York City: Chase Manhattan Bank

New York City: Chemical Bank

New York City: Citibank

Rochester: Security Norstar Bank

New Jersey

Jackson: Garden State Bank

Lodi: National Community Bank of New Jersey

Newark: First Fidelity Bank

North Plainfield: North Plainfield State Bank

Union: The Money Store Investment Corporation

REGION III

Pennsylvania

Erie: Marine Bank

Perkasie: Bucks County Bank & Trust Co.

Pittsburgh: Mellon Bank

Pittsburgh: Pittsburgh National Bank

Reading: Meridian Bank

Virginia

Richmond: Sovran Bank

Richmond: United Virginia Bank

Huntington: First Huntington National Bank

REGION IV

Alabama

Birmingham: Central Bank of the South

Florida

North Miami Beach: First Western SBLC, Inc.

Panama City: Bay Bank & Trust Company

Panama City: First National Bank

Orlando: Sun Bank

Georgia

Atlanta: First National Bank of Atlanta

Atlanta: Fulton Federal Savings

Atlanta: Southern Federal Savings & Loan

Atlanta: Southern National Bank

Atlanta: The Business Development Corp. of Georgia, Inc.

Atlanta: Citizens & Southern National Bank

Augusta: Bankers First Savings & Loan Association

North Carolina

Winston-Salem: Wachovia Bank & Trust Company

South Carolina

Columbia: Bankers Trust of South Carolina

Mississippi

Jackson: Deposit Guaranty National Bank

Tennessee

Elizabethton: Citizens Bank

Memphis: National Bank of Commerce

Memphis: Union Planters National Bank

Nashville: Commerce Union Bank

Nashville: First American National Bank

Nashville: Third National Bank

REGION V

Illinois

Benton: United Illinois Bank of Benton

Chicago: South Shore Bank of Chicago

Joliet: First Midwest Bank

Urbana: Busey First National Bank

Indiana

Fort Wayne: Lincoln National Bank of Fort Wayne

Michigan

Midland: Chemical Bank and Trust Co.

Minnesota

Minneapolis: First National Bank of Minneapolis

St. Cloud: First American Bank of St. Cloud

Ohio

Bowling Green: Mid-America National Bank and Trust Co.

Cincinnati: First National Bank of Cincinnati

Columbus: Bank One of Columbus

Columbus: Huntington National Bank

Dayton: First National Bank of Dayton

Wisconsin

Madison: First Wisconsin National Bank of Madison

Milwaukee: Associates Commerce Bank

Milwaukee: First Wisconsin National Bank of Milwaukee

Milwaukee: M&I Northern Bank

Milwaukee: Marine Bank

Sheboygan: First National Bank of Sheboygan

Wausau: First American National Bank of Wausau

REGION VI

Arkansas

Little Rock: Commercial National Bank of Texarkana

New Mexico

Albuquerque: First National Bank of Albuquerque

Louisiana

Baton Rouge: Capital Bank and Trust Co.

Oklahoma

Stillwater: Stillwater National Bank Trust Co.

Texas

Brownsville: Texas Commerce Bank

Corpus Christi: First National Bank

El Paso: Texas Commerce Bank

El Paso: First City Bank

Houston: Texas American Bank

Longview: Longview Bank & Trust Co.

Lubbock: First National Bank

Seguin: Southwestern Commercial Credit

REGION VII

Iowa

Cedar Rapids: Merchants National Bank of Cedar Rapids

Davenport: Davenport Bank & Trust Co.

Des Moines: Norwest Bank

Sioux City: Security National Bank

Sioux City: Toy National Bank

West Des Moines: West Des State Bank

Kansas

Liberal: First National Bank of Liberal

Merriam: United Kansas Bank & Trust

Wichita: Fourth National Bank & Trust Company

Missouri

Columbia: First National Bank & Trust Company

Jefferson City: Central Trust Company

Kansas City: United Missouri Bank

Springfield: The Boatmen's National Bank

St. Louis: Mercantile Trust Company

Nebraska

Lincoln: First National Bank & Trust Company

Lincoln: Union Bank & Trust Company

REGION VIII

Colorado

Denver: Republic National Bank of Englewood

Denver: Southwestern Commercial Capital, Inc.

Montana

Whitefish: Mountain Bank

South Dakota

Sioux Falls: Western Bank of Sioux Falls

Utah

Salt Lake City: First Security Bank of Utah

Salt Lake City: Tracey Collins Bank & Trust Company

Salt Lake City: Valley Bank & Trust Company

Wyoming

Cheyenne: First Wyoming Bank

REGION IX

Arizona

Phoenix: The Valley National Bank of Arizona

Phoenix: Thunderbird Bank

California

Bakersfield: San Joaquin Bank

Hollywood: American Pacific State Bank

San Luis Obispo: First Bank of San Luis Obispo

San Francisco: Bank of America

San Francisco: Wells Fargo

Hawaii

Honolulu: Bank of Hawaii

Nevada

Las Vegas: Valley Bank of Nevada

REGION X

Alaska

Anchorage: Alaska Pacific Bank

Idaho

Boise: Idaho First National Bank

Washington

Lynwood: City Bank

Seattle: Rainier National Bank

Spokane: Washington Trust Bank

SBA FIELD OFFICES

Alabama
2121 8th Avenue North
Suite 200
Birmingham AL 35203-2398
205/731-1344

Alaska
Room 1068, Module G
8th & C Street
Anchorage AK 99501
907/271-4022

Arizona
2005 North Central Avenue
5th Floor
Phoenix AZ 85004
602/241-3732

Arkansas
320 West Capitol Avenue
Suite 601
Little Rock AR 77201
501/378-5871

California
450 Golden Gate Avenue
Box 36044
San Francisco CA 94102
415/556-4724

211 Main Street
4th Floor
San Francisco CA 94105
415/974-0599

California (cont.)

350 South Figueroa Street
6th Floor
Los Angeles CA 90071
213/894-2956

2202 Monterey Street
Suite 108
Fresno CA 93721
209/487-5189

880 Front Street
Suite 4-S-29
San Diego CA 92188
619/293-7272

660 J Street
Suite 215
Sacramento CA 95814
916/551-1446

Fidelity Federal Building
2700 North Main Street
Suite 400
Santa Ana CA 92701
617/472-2494

Colorado

Executive Tower Building
1405 Curtis Street
22nd Floor
Denver CO 80202-2599
303/844-2607

Connecticut

330 Main Street
2nd Floor
Hartford CT 06106
203/722-3600

Delaware

844 King Street
Room 5297
Lockbox 16
Wilmington DE 19801
302/573-6294

District of Columbia

1111 18th Street NW
Sixth Floor
P.O. Box 19993
Washington DC 20036.
202/634-4850

Florida

400 West Bay Street
Box 35067
Jacksonville FL 32202
904/791-3782

1320 South Dixie Highway
Suite 501
Coral Gables FL 33136
305/536-5521.

700 Twiggs Street
Room 607
Tampa FL 33602
813/228-2594.

3500 45th Street
Suite 6
West Palm Beach FL 33407
305/689-2223

Georgia

1375 Peachtree Street NE
5th Floor
Atlanta GA 30367-8102
404/347-2797

1720 Peachtree Road NW
6th Floor
Atlanta GA 30309
404/347-2441

Federal Building
Room 225
52 North Main Street
Statesboro GA 30458
912/489-8719

Guam

Pacific News Building
Room 508
238 O'Hara Street
Agana, Guam 96910
671/472-7277

Hawaii

300 Ala Moana
Room 2213
P.O. Box 50207
Honolulu HI 96850
808/541-2977

Idaho

1020 Main Street
Suite 290
Boise ID 83702
208/334-1696

Illinois

230 South Dearborn Street
Room 510
Chicago IL 60604
312/523-4528

219 South Dearborn Street
Room 437
Chicago IL 60605
312/353-4528

Washington Building
Four North Old State
Capitol Plaza
Springfield IL 62701
217/492-4416

Indiana

575 North Pennsylvania Street, Room 578
Indianapolis IN 46204-1584
317/269-7272

Iowa

210 Walnut Street
Des Moines IA 50309
515/284-4760

363 Collins Road NE
Cedar Rapids IA 52402
319/399-2571

Kansas

Main Place Building
110 East Waterman Street
Wichita KS 67202
316/269-6191

Kentucky

Federal Office Building
600 Federal Place
Room 188
Louisville KY 40202
502/582-5976

Louisiana

Ford-Fisk Building
1661 Canal Street
2nd Floor
Shreveport LA 71101.
318/589-6685

Maine

40 Western Avenue
Federal Building
Room 512
Augusta ME 04330
207/622-8378

Maryland

10 North Calvert Street
3rd Floor
Baltimore MD 21202
301/962-4392

Massachusetts

60 Batterymarch Street
10th Floor
Boston MA 02110
617/223-3204

Massachusetts (cont.)

10 Causeway Street
Room 265
Boston MA 02114
617/565-5590

Federal Building and Courthouse
1550 Main Street
Room 212
Springfield MA 01103

Michigan

McNamara Building
477 Michigan Avenue, Room 515
Detroit MI 48226
313/226-6075

220 West Washington Street
Marquette MI 49885
906/225-1108

Minnesota

610-C Butler Square
100 North 6th Street
Minneapolis MN 55403
612/349-3574

Mississippi

Dr. A.H. McCoy Federal Building
100 West Capitol Street
Suite 322
Jackson MS 39269

One Hancock Plaza
Suite 1001
Gulfport MS 39501-7758
601/863-4449

Missouri

911 Walnut Street
13th Floor
Kansas City MO 64106
816/374-5868

815 Olive Street
Room 242
St. Louis MO 63101
314/425-6600

339 Broadway
Room 140
Cape Girardeau MO 63701
314/335-6039

The Landmark Building
309 North Jefferson
Springfield MO 65805
417/864-7670

Montana

301 South Park Avenue
Room 528
Drawer 10054
Helena MT 59626
406/449-5381

Post Office Building
Room 216
2601 First Avenue North
Billings MT 59101
406/657-6047

Nebraska

11145 Mill Valley Road
Omaha NE 68154
402/221-4691

Nevada

Box 7257 (Downtown Station)
301 East Stewart
Las Vegas NV 89125
702/388-6019

50 South Virginia Street
Room 238
P.O. Box 3216
Reno NV 89506
702/784-5268

New Hampshire

55 Pleasant Street
Room 209
P.O. Box 1257
Concord NH 03301
603/225-1400, ext. 4402

New Jersey

60 Park Place
4th Floor
Newark NJ 07102
201/645-2434

2600 Mt. Ephrain Avenue
Camden NJ 08104
609/757-5184

New Mexico

Patio Plaza Building
Suite 320
5000 Marble Avenue NE
Albuquerque NM 87110
505/262-6171

New York

26 Federal Plaza
Room 29-118
New York NY 10278
212/264-7772

445 Broadway
Room 236-B
Albany NY 12207
518/472-6300

111 West Huron Street
Room 1311
Buffalo NY 14202
716/846-4301

333 East Water Street
Room 412
Elmira NY 14901
607/734-8130

35 Pinelawn Road
Room 102-E
Melville NY 11747
516/454-0750

Federal Building
Room 601
100 State Street
Rochester NY 14614
716/263-6700

Federal Building
Room 1071
100 South Clinton Street
Syracuse NY 13260
315/423-5383

North Carolina

222 South Church Street
Room 300
Charlotte NC 28202
704/371-6563

North Dakota

Federal Building
Room 218
657 Second Avenue, North
P.O. Box 3086
Fargo ND 58102
701/237-5131

Ohio

AJC Federal Building
Room 317
1240 East 9th Street
Cleveland OH 44199
216/522-4180

Federal Building
U.S. Courthouse
85 Marconi Boulevard
Room 512
Columbus OH 43215
614/469-6860

John Weld Peck Federal Building
550 Main Street
Room 5028
Cincinnati OH 45202
513/684-2814.

Oklahoma

200 NW 5th Street
Suite 670
Oklahoma City OK 73102
405/231-4494

Oregon

Federal Building
Room 676
1220 SW Third Avenue
Portland OR 97204-2882
503/423-5221

Pennsylvania

One Bala Cynwyd Plaza
231 St. Asaphs Road
Suite 640 West
Bala Cynwyd PA 19004
512/596-5889

100 Chestnut Street
Room 309
Harrisburg PA 17101
717/782-3840

960 Penn Avenue
5th Floor
Pittsburgh PA 15222
412/644-2780

Puerto Rico

Federico Degatau Federal Building
Room 691
Carlos Chardon Avenue
Hato Rey, Puerto Rico, 00918
809/753-4002

Rhode Island

380 Westminster Mall
Providence RI 02903
401/528-4586

South Carolina

1835 Assembly Street
3rd Floor
P.O. Box 2786
Columbia SC 29202
803/765-5376.

South Dakota

101 South Main Avenue
Suite 101
Security Building
Sioux Falls SD 57102-0577
605/336-2980, ext. 231

Tennessee

404 James Robertson Parkway
Suite 1012
Parkway Towers
Nashville TN 37219
615/767-7643

Texas

1100 Commerce Street
Dallas TX 75242
214/767-0495

Federal Building
Room 780
300 East 8th Street
Austin TX 78701
512/482-5288

Texas (cont.)

819 Taylor Street
Room 8A32
Fort Worth TX 76102
817/334-3613

400 Mann Street
Suite 403
Corpus Christi TX 78401
512/888-3331

10737 Gateway West
Suite 320
El Paso TX 79935
915/541-7560

222 East Van Buren Street
Suite 500
Harlingen TX 78550
512/888-3331

2525 Murworth
Suite 112
Houston TX 77054
713/660-4420

1611 10th Street
Suite 200
Lubbock TX 79401
806/743-7481

100 South Washington Street
Room G-12
Federal Building
Marshall TX 75670
214/935-5257

Texas (cont.)
Federal Building
Room A-513
727 East Durango Street
San Antonio TX 78206
512/229-6272

Utah
125 South State Street
Room 2237
Salt Lake City UT 84138-1195
801/524-3209.

Vermont
87 State Street
Room 205
Montpelier VT 05602
802/828-4474

Virginia
400 North 8th Street
Room 3015
P.O. Box 10126
Richmond VA 23240
804/771-2765

Virgin Islands
Veterans Drive
Federal Building
Room 210
St. Thomas, Virgin Islands, 00801
809/774-8530

Washington

Fourth & Vine Building
2615 Fourth Avenue
Room 440
Seattle WA 98121
206/442-1456

915 Second Avenue
Room 1792
Seattle WA 98174
206/442-5534

U.S. Courthouse
Room 651
P.O. Box 2167
Spokane WA 99201.

West Virginia

168 West Main Street
5th Floor
Clarksburg WV 26301
304/623-5631

550 Eagan Street
Room 309
Charleston WV 25301
304/347-5220

Wisconsin

212 East Washington Avenue
Room 213
Madison WI 53703
608/264-5205

Henry S. Reuss Federal Plaza
310 West Wisconsin Avenue
Suite 400
Milwaukee WI 53203
414/291-3942

Wisconsin (cont.)

Federal Office Building & U.S. Courthouse
500 South Barstow Street
Room 17
Eau Claire WI 54701
715/834-9012

Wyoming

100 East B Street
Federal Building
Room 4001
P.O. Box 2839
Casper WY 82602-2839.
307/261-5761

COLD CALLING TECHNIQUES
(That <u>Really</u> Work!)

by Stephan Schiffman

You smoke a cigarette . . . wander by the water cooler . . . glance at the clock on the wall . . . and realize that the time has come. You look at the phone, slowly lift the receiver, and face a salesperson's greatest dread: the cold call.

If you're a salesperson faced with the constant, bewildering problem of "getting those appointments," you know how difficult it can be to turn a list of names and phone numbers into a calendar filled with solid prospects waiting to meet you. It can be done, and COLD CALLING TECHNIQUES offers a comprehensive and proven six-week plan that can make the cold call an opportunity, not a chore, for novice and veteran alike.

By following the plan that's worked for thousands of salespeople at top companies, you will:

- Discover the one simple phrase that can turn around the vast majority of all objections
- Learn how to be your own sales manager
- Find out how to monitor your calls and set goals based on your personal statistics
- Determine exactly how much time per week you should allot to cold calling
- See how business is like war - and what exactly your role is on the battlefield.

COLD CALLING TECHNIQUES (That <u>Really</u> Work!) will change a salesperson's attitude about the cold call, about personal goals, about sales as a profession, and will show the way for every salesperson to make a lot more money. Take the challenge to become more effective on the phone, more productive in your schedule, and more likely to land sales.

Stephan Shiffman is President of D.E.I. Management Group, Inc., a sales training firm. He has successfully trained nearly 200,000 salespeople for such companies as AT&T, Honeywell, and Prudential-Bache.

Paperback, 6" x 9" ● $6.95

ORDER TOLL FREE
1-800-872-5627
In MA: 617-268-9570

Or send $6.95 + $2.75 shipping and handling to:

*BOB ADAMS, INC.
260 CENTER STREET
HOLBROOK, MA 02343*